Delmar,

I cannot even
you how thankful I
Your friendship. Thank you for
all of your advice you gave
me in the writing of this
book.

AKA - "NICK"

"Amazing"
My Long, Dark, and Sometimes Hilarious Journey To
Sobriety

By Nicholas Myra

"I am a mother; Nick's mother. I am also an educator. Nick's story opened my eyes to gives with addictions. There is a way out. I would recommend this book to parents and students, especially junior high students. I pray that other parents might do better than I did at recognizing a child who is caught in the snare of this terrible disease."
        -Nick's Mother

"I am currently finishing my Ph.D. in clinical psychology and the author's brother. Reading about my brother's struggle with alcohol and subsequent life of recovery provided me with a glimpse of the devastation caused by alcohol and the hardships one must overcome when choosing a sober life. I believe this book should be read by anyone struggling with alcohol or other addictions as well as those who have loved ones with such addictions."
        Nick's Brother

Amazing left me laughing and crying as I discovered just how life as an alcoholic can be. This book will change the life of the twelve year old who will soon encounter peer pressure. It will change the life of the mother who has an alcoholic daughter. It will inspire the man who is locked in the vicious cell of alcoholism. This book will inspire everyone who picks it up. This book has a power to change your life.
-teenager and former member of Nick's youth group

Too many persons suffering with the disease of alcoholism, reject their faith rather than relying on it as a source for sustained recovery. Nicholas has changed the lives of dozens of teens with his commitment to love and support them where they are. In his own journey, I have seen him

relate to his God in the same way-knowing that he is embraced and loved just as he is, a man with the disease of alcoholism. His book demonstrates the open door faith can provide anyone searching to be made whole. As an addictions specialist, I heartily recommend this book.
-Social Worker

"I am a Roman Catholic Priest. I found this book to be helpful on many levels. It very seriously and openly addresses the issues of alcoholism, but it also does much more than that. It is about a journey through life and many lessons learned. Therefore it can be valuable to everyone.
The book includes some very important themes: Freedom, Forgiveness, Honesty, Accountability, Peace, etc. These are key themes for anyone who is serious about this journey that we call life."
-Catholic Priest

"After working 32 years in Veterans Medical Centers as a Kinesiotherapist in the Physical Medicine and Rehabilitation Department, 29 of those years directly with Veterans within the SARP (Substance Abuse Rehabilitation Program), I have an intimate understanding of the effects of Substance Abuse. I am currently an Ordained Catholic Deacon with a hospital based ministry and I often come in contact with individuals suffering from alcoholism and poly drug addiction.
Amazing is ones journey through a life of alcohol addiction. One could almost leave all the names blank and fill in the blanks with names of those you know and possibly yourself. It addresses addiction in the real world and in real situations.

The use of the "Beatitudes" and integrating them into the "12 Steps" is unique and gives a refreshing twist to how our Higher Power and Spirituality work together in coming to grips and dealing with ones addiction.

Amazing is one of those books that can be used within the full spectrum of those individuals who deal with addiction in their life."

   -Catholic Deacon

"While this book is captivating and seamlessly engaging as to be read cover-to-cover in one sitting, it would be immensely valuable for the reader to then take a second read, just one chapter or even one paragraph at a time and use it as a template to write his own story. This book challenges the stereotypes and rationalizations associated with addiction and expose the TRUTH with courage and tremendous heart."

   -Catholic Youth Minister

This book is dedicated to my wife. Thank you for seeing the best in me. Thank you for sticking with me. Thank you for loving me. You are my best friend. You always have and always will make me a better person. I love you.

Thank You.
There are several people that deserve my gratitude for the help they gave me in writing this book. Because of anonymity, I cannot name them personally.
Nevertheless, I wish to thank the people who read this book as I completed each chapter and advised me along the way.
You know who you are, THANK YOU.

First Things First

One of the most important traditions in Alcoholics Anonymous is that of anonymity. Although the stories in this book are true, I have changed the names of people including my own (my name is not Nicholas Myra) and locations in order to protect the tradition of anonymity as well as the privacy of the people who have been a part of my life. With that being said, there are many who will read this book and will know that I wrote it. Whether you know me or not, the following letters are for you.

To the normal reader:

This is a book about addiction and addiction is very ugly. There is nothing glamorous about alcoholism. If you are offended easily, I would not recommend reading this book. Many people have advised me against including some of the more "graphic" stories. However, I feel that, if I'm going to tell a story, I should tell it like it is. That being said, I do want to reassure the reader that there are no pornographic stories or anything like that, although there is some profanity. I take the liberty on more than one occasion of expressing some pretty strong opinions. If this book were a movie, it would probably be rated PG-13. I personally feel that it is okay for teens to read this book, but I would not recommend it for middle-school aged youth.

To my family:

As you read this, your feelings may be hurt by some of the things I write about. My intentions are not to hurt you, but to tell the truth. In doing this, it is my hope that others can see that problems should not be ignored, no matter how difficult they may be to confront. Maybe, by writing this book, I can open up lines of communication that should have been opened years ago. I love you all and hope that this book brings us closer together rather than farther apart.

To the recovering alcoholic:
    I pray that you will find this book to be a source of motivation to continue on your road to recovery. I hope that this book can be a tool that you can give to friends or family who may be suffering from the disease of alcoholism. I pray that you will laugh as you recognize how similar our experiences are and I pray that we can celebrate our recovery together through our common bond of sobriety.

To the alcoholic who is still drinking:
    I pray for you daily. May you read this book and realize that you are not alone. I pray that you will laugh. I pray that you will cry. Above all, I pray that you will read this book and find hope.

To all the teens I have worked with or will work with:
    I pray that you will learn from my mistakes and should you ever repeat them, I will find you and beat you severely—no, just kidding! I truly hope that you can see my mistakes for what they are and, in reading this book, understand even more fully how much God loves you.

Higher Power

One of the main elements of recovery is belief in a Higher Power. In this book and in my life, I choose to call my Higher Power "God". I am a Roman Catholic and therefore, my recovery experiences are intertwined with my Catholic faith. However, this book is not just for Catholics/Christians or a book on Catholic theology. I do tell some stories and make some references to Catholic things, but it is not my intention to convert you, the reader, to Catholicism. The stories and references that I've included are simply a part of my story. They are in no way meant to represent or promote the teachings of the Roman Catholic Church. AA does not endorse any particular religious denomination, but welcomes people of any faith or no faith.

It doesn't matter what name you choose to give your Higher Power. In fact, in different parts of this book, I use "God" and "Jesus" interchangeably with "Higher Power". I wanted to give you, the reader, a "heads up" on this because I have met many people who had terrible experiences in a church of some sort. A number of them suffered unbelievable guilt and judgment, or even physical/sexual abuse, at the hands of people claiming to be acting or speaking for "God". The last thing I want to have happen is for someone to start to read this book and then put it down as soon as they come to the word "God" or "Jesus". As I have already stated, I don't care what name you give to your Higher Power. You are free to choose and, if you choose a different name than I do, it does not mean that your experiences are any less real. Please extend me the same courtesy.

Amazing ~Nicholas Myra

Published by LeClere Books
P. O. Box 27890
St. Louis, MO 63146
314-808-4136
Leclerebooks.com

Cover Design: Brandi Kapfer
Book Layout: Bonnie Allen
Editor: Gary Darby
Page 15 Illustration: M. Slater

Printed by Lightning Source, Inc
Manufactured in the United States of America

ISBN 9780984315826

The 12 Steps of Alcoholics Anonymous*

1. We admitted we were powerless over alcohol, that our lives had become unmanageable;
2. Came to believe that a Power greater than ourselves could restore us to sanity;
3. Made a decision to turn our will and our lives over to the care of God as we understood Him;
4. Made a searching and fearless moral inventory of ourselves;
5. Admitted to God, to ourselves and to another human being the exact nature of our wrongs;
6. Were entirely ready to have God remove all these defects of character;
7. Humbly asked Him to remove our shortcomings;
8. Made a list of all persons we had harmed, and became willing to make amends to them all;
9. Made direct amends to such people wherever possible, except when to do so would injure them or others;
10. Continued to take personal inventory, and when we were wrong, promptly admitted it;
11. Sought through prayer and meditation to improve our conscious contact with God, as we understood Him, praying only for knowledge of His will for us and the power to carry that out.
12. Having had a spiritual awakening as the result of these steps, we tried to carry this message to alcoholics, and to practice these principles in all our affairs.

contents of this publication, or that AAWS necessarily agrees with the views expressed herein. A.A. is a program of recovery from alcoholism only - use of the Twelve Steps in connection with programs and activities which are patterned after A.A., but which address other problems, or in any other non-A.A. context, does not imply otherwise. Additionally, while A.A. is a spiritual program, A.A. is not a religious program. Thus, A.A. is not affiliated or allied with any sect, denomination, or specific religious belief.

Table of Contents

Chapter I

Step One: We admitted we were powerless over alcohol, that our lives had become unmanageable.

The pain of my addiction climaxed on a Sunday night in March, when I suddenly came to the stark realization that my life was at a crossroads. I knew that I had to make a change; I had a decision to make. It was time to confront my drinking head on. Although God would later help me to recover, I knew that the demon of alcoholism was something that I would have to face alone. I had been kidding myself about my drinking far too long.

Coming to a place where you can admit that you are powerless over alcohol happens in different ways for different people. For some, it takes a huge wake-up call, like losing a spouse or getting arrested. For others, it may come in the form of health problems or losing money. No matter what the circumstances, it always involves pain of one kind or another. Pain reminds us we are alive and sometimes acts as a warning signal, telling us that it is time to make a change.

I was a high-functioning alcoholic. I had to be in order to do the work I enjoyed. I have spent most of my adult life working with teenagers and youth groups. I wish that I could say that I was able to overcome my addiction early in my career as a youth worker, but that would be untrue.

The real truth is that, during all of the years I spent working with teens in detention centers, youth centers, group homes, and churches, I was an alcoholic. Many people I worked with knew that I drank and that I sometimes drank too much. However, very few people knew how serious my drinking problem was. My co-workers who *did* were people that drank with me.

In fact, a good friend and drinking buddy of mine named Bret had worked with me for several years at a juvenile detention center. Strangely enough, I had helped Bret get the job at the detention center after *Second Chance*, the alcohol treatment center where he had been working, closed down.

Bret was my favorite drinking buddy. During our years working at the detention center together, both of us also played in popular local rock bands and worked full-time during the day. I was a drummer in my band and Bret was a drummer and lead singer in his. I can't remember how many times we played on a Friday night, drank until three or four o'clock in the morning, and then came into work to supervise teens at seven o'clock, only three hours later on the same day.

I'll never forget one such night when my band was playing at a popular bar in town. Bret was there, along with another detention staff member named Donna who had also worked at *Second Chance*. Donna was there celebrating her birthday with her husband and some friends. Bret was extremely drunk (as was I) and he decided that he wanted to sing happy birthday to Donna since they were "old friends." In between songs, Bret jumped onto the stage and, with a beer in one hand and a microphone in the other he explained to the crowd what a great lady Donna was and that it was her birthday. He told everybody that he had known Donna ever since they had worked together at *Second Chance* (you know, the *ALCOHOL TREATMENT CENTER*). Then he pointed at me behind the drums and said, "Now we both work together, along with Nick, at the juvenile detention center."

When Bret had finished his drunken ramblings, someone in the audience yelled, "No wonder that place closed down. It was being run by a bunch of drunks!" The bar erupted with laughter and my band began the next song.

The following day, we were all at work at the detention center at seven o'clock in the morning and on Sunday I was at church working with the kids. In my mind, it had been just another normal weekend.

This kind of behavior continued for years because of my ability to lead two separate lives. There was a crowd of drinkers that knew me as a wild, drunken drummer who was always doing something crazy. However, they had no idea what I did when I wasn't drinking or playing music in a bar.

Then there were the people who attended my church and the people with whom I worked who viewed me as responsible and stable. They knew I played music and drank sometimes, but they had no idea what I was really like when the sun went down.

I think that the secrecy of my alcoholism is what allowed it to continue for so long. I had never been in trouble with the law although I came close several times. I always had a job and I never drank at work. I did not feel that my life was unmanageable, even though most of my time was spent trying to manage my life so that I could continue to drink with complete abandon while keeping up appearances where necessary.

When I became a full-time youth minister in 2003, I thought that would slow my drinking down. All it did, however, was cause me to resort to more clever measures to hide my addiction. I almost always drank alone at home or at social functions where *everyone* was drinking, so I wouldn't look out of place.

If I attended any event where only a few people were drinking, I would get drunk beforehand and then take my own flask of whiskey to drink in the bathroom. I was able to function very well when drunk. There were times that even my wife could not tell how much I had had to drink.

I'm certain that the high visibility that was associated with my job working with teens only helped to prevent me from confronting my problem. What would people say if they found out that the man working so hard to provide a positive influence in the spiritual lives of their kids was a drunk?

My own pride and my concern for what other people might think had become a roadblock to recovery. Besides, for me to admit that I had a drinking problem would mean admitting that I had a problem with my own spirituality. I didn't know if I was ready to do that.

Sometimes I wonder how many church members or pastors out there have serious drinking or drug problems, but are afraid to seek help because of what other people might think. Churches need to start taking better care of their members who have addictions. Instead of crucifying them or shaming them when they come forward for help, they need to welcome them in the way Jesus would have and help them find a road to their recovery.

Often, in churches, the addict or alcoholic is treated as a modern-day leper. This may be because churchgoers are afraid to recognize that a member of their congregation has an addiction because this might mean their church as a whole or that they personally had somehow failed. This, of course, is not true. A church only fails if it pretends that its members are perfect and that they don't have any problems.

I would be willing to bet that every church in this nation has at least one alcoholic in its congregation. It is also very likely that at least one in five churches has an alcoholic on its staff. I don't have any statistics to back this up, but when you look at the total number of addicts in our nation, this becomes a real possibility.

There are far too many people who think that only people like convicts and the homeless are alcoholics. These are dangerous stereotypes. Many different people from all walks of life suffer from this disease and many of them go to church.

After becoming a youth minister, I tried to live as a devout Catholic and did my best to sell myself as exactly that to everyone I came into contact with. Admitting that I was spiritually sick might be too painful, not to mention the fact that it would mean admitting my own human weakness.

I hated the thought of admitting that I wasn't strong enough to handle something by myself. Besides, I was living a pretty good life as far as most people could see. I recognized that there had been times in my life that I drank too much, but now I prayed and went to church. In many ways I was a different person.

I wasn't hanging out in bars on the weekends or staying out all night partying like a rock star after a gig with my band while my wife was at home in bed. That had all ended years ago. For crying out loud, I was working with teens and teaching them about God now! Hadn't I atoned for my sins? I knew I was an alcoholic in the traditional sense of the word, but if I could function okay as an alcoholic, then what was the big deal? Nobody's perfect, right?

Many of these things went through my mind as I knelt on the kitchen floor that night in March, trying to catch my breath after throwing up. I had forced myself to throw up so that I could drink more. Bulimia was something I had learned to practice in my late teens, although it came and went, depending on the intensity of my drinking. I no longer used it for weight management, but it came in handy when I was full of beer and wanted to continue drinking.

The house was empty, except for my two dogs. My wife was out of town. It was ten o'clock on a Sunday night and I had already consumed more than a case of beer. The only light in the house came from the living room where an old 80's movie was playing on the TV with the sound turned off. Leaning against the cabinets with my hand on the sink, I felt empty, alone and worthless.

This was not the first time in my drinking "career" that I had felt this way and I was certainly no stranger to puking as a result of drinking. I had said my share of prayers into the toilet bowl. They were always prayers full of empty promises and false resolve.

But, that night, I didn't pray. I didn't promise anything to anyone, not even myself. I was done making empty promises to God and to others that I wouldn't be able to keep. I just wanted it all to stop and I didn't care how or why. Dying would work just fine. I didn't care, as long as I *didn't have to drink anymore.*

Then I remembered something that I had heard at one of the AA meetings that I had attended in the past to appease my wife. That night I remembered the word "Powerless."

It's interesting how God has a way of bringing us to our knees in spite of ourselves.

I had never thought of myself as being "powerless." I loved to drink and I liked the taste. I liked the feeling of intoxication. I enjoyed the many good times I had with friends while drinking.

And yes—newsflash, folks—there *were* good times. They weren't *all* good, but nevertheless, good times did abound. Some may find this shocking. Straight-laced teetotalers may read this and scream out, "BLASPHEMY!" But I cannot deny that I had many good memories that involved more than a little alcohol.

To understand how this could be, you have to remember that, for someone like me who started drinking at the age of fifteen and continued almost non-stop for sixteen years, alcohol was *always* there. In fact, there were only two times in my life when I had quit drinking for a short time.

One was during my first nine months in the United States Marine Corps and the second was during the first eight months of my first marriage. Of course, even though the alcohol wasn't present during either of these times, the black and white behavior that accompanies alcoholism was.

I think I may have burned as many bridges during those sixteen "dry" months as I had over the years I was drinking.

For over half of my life, alcohol was as familiar a presence as underwear (of course, in later stories involving my alcoholism, underwear was conspicuously absent, but I'm getting ahead of myself). Alcohol was my constant companion. I was married to it but even the worst marriages have some good memories.

It would be asinine to think that an alcoholic could not ever have fun or do anything good. At least once a month (and sometimes once a week), I receive phone calls and letters from teens that I have worked with, telling me how much I helped them in their own struggles. Most of these letters are from teens I worked with during some of my own worst times. Many alcoholics are great at helping others; they just don't do too well at helping themselves. I was a perfect example of this.

Too often, people in society (especially "church people") place tons of undue guilt on alcoholics by trying to convince them that admitting to having had any fun while drinking is a serious sin. This creates the belief in alcoholics that they never accomplished anything good and were totally worthless all the years they were drinking. What kind of incentive does that provide for an alcoholic to quit drinking?

Who in their right mind would want to face the realization that their entire life, until the day they became sober, had been utterly destitute of anything good? God can use us for good in spite of ourselves. The countless phone calls and letters I receive from teens whose lives I have impacted are evidence that my life wasn't *all* bad during my drinking years.

Of course, we should never use God's mercy as an excuse to continue a destructive lifestyle. However, to say that God has no use for addicts is to assume that there is a limit to His power. And if you are going to limit the power of God, then what hope is there for recovery?

The God who helps us recover is the same God who loves us through our darkest times. And if there is one thing all alcoholics can agree on, it is that there are some very dark times. There are times that are so dark, hopeless and painful that you cannot even remember a time that you lived differently.

We become so paralyzed by our addiction that we can see no way out. However, as alcoholics in recovery, we know that if we are truly changed people who have found a new way, we should never be ashamed of our past. My past does not scare me anymore. It is, instead, an open book that you now hold in your hands. My future is yet to be written.

Alcohol was always there because I *wanted* it there. Sometimes I even referred to myself as a "professional alcoholic." However, I started to get scared when I began having days when I didn't want to drink, but I wasn't able to stop myself. There were days when I would become physically ill at the thought of drinking.

Nevertheless, I would be at the store that afternoon, buying a case of beer on my way home. Weekend after weekend, when my wife was out of town, I would try to plan activities for myself other than drinking. It never quite worked out and I would always end up drunk, anyway.

The last year I drank, I would drink until I physically couldn't put any more alcohol in my body because I was "full." Five or six nights a week I would drink at least a case of beer or a bottle of whiskey and then I would force myself to vomit so that I could continue drinking. It was one of these nights that brought me to my knees in our kitchen with the word "powerless" in my head.[*]

---

[*] On a side note, this is not a book about self-esteem, although I think it is important to mention that a large number of alcoholics deal with low self-esteem and eating disorders. I was no exception. As a kid, I was always a bit overweight—not obese, mind you, but certainly not

Looking back at my life, I have to admit that from the time I started drinking, virtually every memory I had, whether good or bad, was influenced by the presence or the absence of alcohol. Good times were great because of alcohol and bad times were horrible because of alcohol.

Sometimes, alcohol made good times better and bad times worse. On other occasions, it made bad times better and good times worse. Either way, alcohol was the common denominator. If I was successful, I celebrated with alcohol. If I failed, I medicated with alcohol. If I worked hard, I rewarded myself with alcohol. If I didn't work to my potential, I eased my mind with alcohol. If alcohol wasn't, or couldn't be, a part of something I was doing, I didn't want to do it.

---

lean. I remember my dad screaming at me to "suck it in, for Christ's sake" when I was trying on jeans in the department store and couldn't button them.

I struggled with my weight for a long time, and when I discovered bulimia, I thought it was great. I could eat all I wanted and then throw it up and feel okay again. It also came in handy when I was drinking. I could drink indefinitely, as long as I could make occasional trips to the bathroom.

During my last three or four years of drinking, I began putting on more weight, so the purging became more frequent. Many nights I would see myself in the mirror and become disgusted with my image. I would have to drink until I felt okay enough about myself to eat. Of course, then I would throw it up because I felt guilty. Even at my leanest times, like when I was competing in boxing and weighed a modest 156 pounds, or when I was playing in a rock band and everyone was telling me I looked great and I had girls hitting on me right and left, I still looked in the mirror and saw the little fat kid I used to be.

This distorted view of my body didn't cause my drinking, but it certainly didn't help. Today, I still sometimes see that kid in the mirror, but I am learning to love him because he is me. As I write this book, I currently weigh about 200 pounds and my wife describes me as "sexy and buffed." I don't know if that is how I look to others, but what I do know is that I no longer base my own self-worth or the worth of others on appearances.

If I was forced into participating in a non-alcoholic event by my wife or my family, I went determined to have a bad time and ruin it for everybody else. Then, as soon as it was over, I would reward myself with alcohol for getting through another pointless activity that had no value, simply because alcohol was absent. I can remember swinging by the store at one o'clock in the morning on the way home for a case of beer after many such ridiculous activities.

Powerless? Never!

For me, just like so many other alcoholics before me, it took Divine intervention to realize just how powerless over alcohol I really was. I will never forget that night on March 13th, when God spoke to me as I knelt on the floor with vomit dripping from my lips. He said, "Nick, enough is enough. It is time to quit."

Say what you will about God; I know He is real because He saved my life.

Throughout my whole life, religious zealots have lied to me about how God works, about whom He will help and about how you can find Him. When God saved my life, it didn't happen in any of the ways that a lot of people have tried to make me believe.

Furthermore, there is a huge difference between someone who has "intellectual knowledge" of God and someone who has actual belief in God that comes from a spiritual awakening. Anyone can *agree* that God exists (even the devil agrees that God exists). Intellectual assent that there is "a god" is no big deal for the majority of people.

However, it takes a *spiritual awakening* to experience God in a life-changing way. Recovery is about spiritual experiences that change lives, not about "knowledge" of God. I, for one, have had my fill of unspiritual people pushing their own flavor of religious "knowledge" on me through guilt and manipulation.

I was raised in the Church of Jesus Christ of Latter-Day Saints (Mormons) and was taught for eighteen years that the Mormon Church was the only true church. If recovery has taught me anything, it is that God is bigger than any one church. If anyone is reading this book and has been told that they can only find God in one particular church, then I want you to know that you are being lied to.

I once heard someone tell me that the Twelve Steps are like the "Gospel for dummies." After weighing my experiences in AA against those of many churches I have attended, I have to admit that I have met just as many spiritual people in AA meetings as I have in any church.

I have watched "church people" use God as an excuse for lies, violence, and manipulation. I have witnessed all kinds of revivals that were financially motivated. I have questioned the many different pastors I have met through the years and have found that if I asked ten different pastors the same question; I would receive ten different responses.

Aside from some major theological reasons, I came to the Catholic Church because the Catholics (specifically a Catholic priest named Fr. Juan) took me as I was addiction and all. Initially, my wife accused me of becoming Catholic because they believed it was okay to drink excessively.

I have to admit that I had that misconception about Catholics, as well. However, I have since learned otherwise. If Catholicism teaches anything, it teaches accountability, even if the members don't always live up to the expectations set by the Church (myself being a great example). Through the example and teaching of Fr. Juan, I learned that God seeks us out and rescues us when we need Him most, and He sometimes uses other people to do it.

It is important to remember this when we get to the final stages of recovery, when we must be ready to serve others and carry the message of recovery to those who need it.

The first year I was a Catholic, I ended up in a hospital for a week due to depression related to my alcoholism. Fr. Juan visited me every morning. We talked a lot about my drinking and my duplicate lifestyle. He didn't judge me or condemn me. He didn't shame me or threaten to kick me out. He just told me how much we all matter to God and that we are all important to God and that God will go to any length to find us, because *He made us all.* Fr. Juan's willingness to spend a couple hours with me every day, despite his busy schedule, taught me a lot about compassion.

I can honestly say that now (years later) I understand that no matter where we live or what color we are, God made us. Whether we kneel before a crucifix or bow toward Mecca, God made us. Whether we are brown or white, God made us. Whether we are American or Mexican, God made us.

All life comes from God, so all life *matters* to God. *I matter to God!* For the first time in my life, someone at a church had told me that I mattered. It was not that only Americans mattered or that only members of a particular church mattered, but that all of us are important.

At the time, I still didn't believe it. I couldn't believe it because I was convinced that most of my life had been worthless. But I guess the important thing is that I *wanted* to believe it and that is what planted the seed of self-worth that would later grow and develop with God's prompting.

It would take a bit more pain and six more years of darkness before God would decide to show me how much I mattered to Him. He waited until March 13, 2005, to show me again how important I was to Him. On that night, He didn't send an angel or a priest. Instead, He came Himself.

On an average, unspectacular night in March, God came to me when I was at my worst, and He saved my life. God came to me so that I could experience Him for myself, not because I was a good boy and not because I screamed out in desperation and asked Him to.

He did not come to me because I raised my hand in some church and asked Him into my heart and not because I read the Bible. It was not because the missionaries came to my house, not because I spoke in tongues, not because I was "born again" and not because some preacher laid his hands on me. I didn't go to God that night. God *came to me*, uninvited, and saved my life because He felt that I was worth it.

Do you understand how huge this is? He saw my pain and cared so much that HE CAME TO ME! The realization that I was "worth it" is what gave me the courage I needed to face my alcoholism. In many ways, that is all God had to do. I just needed to hear from Him that I mattered.

Before that moment, my relationship with God had never been much more than lukewarm. I believed, but didn't care to understand. I had leaned on God several times, but how much can you trust Him if you don't trust Him enough to ask for help with your greatest problem? How much faith can you have if, every time you talk to the creator of the universe, you conspicuously avoid bringing up your biggest sickness?

Later, my sponsor would explain to me that I had a "hole in my God-boat." In other words, there was something in my belief about God that caused me to put limits on His power and no amount of "knowledge" about Him could take the place of *experiencing* Him. Why *else* had I not asked Him for help? Did I think that He wasn't powerful enough to help me, or did I believe that I wasn't worth helping?

That night in March, God saved my life by telling me that I was worth it. That was when I realized that I was powerless over alcohol. That was my spiritual awakening. It was my first real moment of clarity.

Many people have asked me to describe what it is like to have a "spiritual awakening." I have struggled with finding the words to describe it. The best I can do is to say that on that night in March, I knew I was going to be alright. That's it. I know that sounds pretty simple but you have no idea what that feels like until you experience it! Tears came to my eyes and I knew that I was worth it. I was going to be alright because God told me so.

Anyone who is reading this and is struggling with an addiction, in case you have never heard it, I want you to know that you are worth it, too. God is there; He is real and He is seeking you now, this very moment. He is powerful when you are powerless. He is waiting for you to admit your own weakness so that He can help you get to work on a new way of living.

Don't wait until you are on your knees and ready to die. Decide right now that you are powerless over whatever you are pouring down your throat or shooting into your arm. It is the first step—and the hardest step—but it is necessary. Do it and rest assured that better days are coming. In the meantime, I, along with many recovering alcoholics around the world, will be saying a prayer for you tonight.

The best I can do is to say that on that night, I knew I was going to be alright.

Chapter II

Step Two: [We] came to believe that a power greater than ourselves could restore us to sanity.

I once heard insanity defined as doing the same thing over and over again and expecting to get a different result. I'm not sure how I would apply that definition to an alcoholic like myself, one who never expected to get different results from drinking. I drank because I wanted the effects of alcohol. I was even willing to put up with the *negative* consequences because I felt the "rush" was worth it. For me, the insanity of my addiction had much more to do with the way alcohol influenced my behavior, even when I wasn't drunk, than what I expected to get from it.

I was a slave to alcohol. Whether I was drinking or not, alcohol was the factor that determined my actions. There had been times when I took a break from drinking in order to get friends and family off my back, but I always intended to start drinking again once everyone had calmed down.

On one occasion, I quit drinking for almost a year during my first marriage, but the disease was still there. It was hiding under the surface and manifesting itself in other ways, such as mood swings, depression, binging and purging, anger, etc.

My first marriage ended due, in large part, to the behaviors that are characteristic of an alcoholic, yet I only drank heavily during the last four months of our fourteen-month marriage! Even without the alcohol, I was still an alcoholic! How could this be? Isn't the alcohol itself the problem?

When I joined AA, my sponsor talked to me for a long time about how much power alcohol had over me and how much it had influenced my life. He explained that I didn't know how to do *anything* sober and that I would have to relearn everything.

I was a bit surprised by this statement. I tried to argue with him about it, but the more we talked and the more I honestly looked at my life, the more I began to realize that alcohol, whether it was in my system or not, was the power that controlled me. Even during those times that I took a break from drinking, I still behaved like an alcoholic.

I was impossible to be around because I couldn't have my "fix." I obsessed over when I would be able to start drinking again. I was irritable and grumpy. I would slip into deep depressions and then jump into periods marked by extreme highs. During these high periods, I would binge on exercise, food, sex or anything else that might take the place of alcohol. If I couldn't drink to excess, then I would find something else to immerse myself in that I could carry beyond the point of moderation.

I stated earlier that I probably burned more bridges with people during my "dry" periods than I did during my drinking times and I meant it. I was unable to live life without alcohol. I couldn't deal with the structure, the problems, or the boredom of reality. I have heard it said many times in recovery meetings that the Twelve Steps have more to do with teaching you how to live than they have to do with alcohol itself.

As I have worked the steps, I have found this to be true. Of the Twelve Steps, only one of them mentions alcohol. The rest are about recovery and how to live sober.

You might be wondering what the difference is between "living sober" and just "not drinking." On my fridge in my kitchen, I have a sign that says the following:

Son
Of a
Bitch

Everything's Real

I can't remember where I first saw this sign, but it reminds me that I have reached the point where I can face reality without the aid of alcohol. I am sober; I am not just taking a break from drinking for a while.

I no longer need to use alcohol as a crutch to help me face reality or as a magic carpet to periodically take me away from real life. I can face life every day without the help of alcohol and, if something gets too big for me to handle alone, I can turn to God instead. My life is no longer characterized by insanity. Rather, it is now filled with serenity and is driven by peace.

Like all recovering alcoholics, I have many stories that show how irrationally and ridiculously I had behaved while drinking. The stories themselves all share that common element of dark humor for the person who has experienced an addiction. However, for someone who has no connection to the disease of alcoholism, the stories may seem far-fetched and even hard to believe. However, I assure you that they are true.

One story in particular comes to mind. There is a pub called Murphy's that I used to frequent in the downtown section of my hometown. During my drinking days, I spent at least three nights a week there, sometimes more.

I knew the bartenders so well that I rarely paid my full tab and quite often I drank for free. So strong was my attachment to this place that, after my wife and I moved to another city located about two-and-a-half hours away, I would take trips back home just to drink at Murphy's. This continued for years, even though most of the regulars I had known there were no longer patrons. I knew I could still drink my fill and spend practically nothing.

Many times during the holidays, when my wife and I would travel home to visit family, I would go straight to the pub as soon as we came into town. I loved Murphy's so much that I wouldn't even go unload my suitcases and say hello to family.

I would just have my wife drive straight from the freeway exit to drop me off at the pub before she went on to the home of whichever relative we were staying with. My friends would know that I was in town because, when they got home from work, they would see the name of the pub on their caller ID. I wouldn't even have to leave a message. They would just know that I was there waiting for them at Murphy's.

If they didn't come down to have a few beers with me, then they could expect phone calls from me throughout the night. The calls would become more belligerent the later it got. Just imagine me sitting at the bar holding a pint of Stout and screaming into the phone, "I don't care if it is your son's birthday. Get your ass down here!"

It was also a common practice on trips to my hometown for me to swing by one of the truck stops along the freeway and buy a couple of quarts of beer to drink while driving the last thirty miles to town. That way, I could have a good buzz going before I got to Murphy's. Only an alcoholic would buy beer to drink on his way to a place where he could practically drink for free. I would label this behavior as insane. At the time, however, I thought it was normal.

One day, shortly after my current wife and I were engaged to be married, Bret and I went to Murphy's right after our shift ended at the detention center at around three o'clock on a Friday afternoon. We spent about three hours there, drinking and laughing.

After we had each consumed enough alcohol to kill any normal person of comparable size and weight, we decided it was time to head down the street to another bar for some shots. We spent about two hours drinking shots of tequila at the second bar before heading to yet another destination. We ended up at a well-known local bar and grill, where we continued our drinking marathon.

We grew weary of beer early in the night and moved on to margaritas. Bret had never tried a watermelon margarita, so I bought one for him. He liked it so much that he ordered a whole pitcher (if one is good, then ten are better). Of course at this point, we couldn't taste the alcohol anymore and this angered Bret. He wanted the drinks to be stronger. So he began negotiating with the bartender and eventually ended up paying the bartender $20.00 to pour tequila into the pitcher of margaritas for seven seconds without stopping.

This caused the margaritas to change color from dark green to a pale, sickly yellow color (later that night we both began to turn that color as well). We drank the "enhanced" margaritas like they were water and, as the night progressed, things gradually went downhill.

At one point, I threatened to break a bottle over the head of some guy that Bret didn't like and then stab him in the throat with it (the bottle). Fortunately, the booze calmed everybody down and soon Bret's "friend" had joined us at the bar. I could see Bret talking to him, but I couldn't hear what they were talking about and didn't care because I didn't even know him. It seemed like they were getting along great, only later I found out that Bret was trying to convince him to go outside and fight me. Wow! With friends like that, who needs enemies?

Around midnight, my girlfriend Beth (now my wife) called me. She didn't call to check on me and she didn't call to get mad at me or offer to drive me home. She just called to say goodnight and tell me that she loved me. Assuming that Beth was calling to check on me, I became angry and started an argument on the phone with her.

I don't remember what was said, but I do remember that I was being an asshole. She became angry with me and started to argue. Next, my loyal friend Bret decided that somehow his drunken comments could help the situation, so he blurted out, "Are you talking to Beth? Is she giving you shit? Let me talk to the bitch."

Because it is impossible for drunks to talk quietly, Beth heard Bret's drunken outbursts in the background and, of course, they made her mad. She insisted on talking to Bret to give him a piece of her mind. I refused to put him on the phone and in an effort to smooth things over; I started yelling at Bret to shut up.

Bret responded by trying to tell me how much he cared about me as a friend and launched into a long, incomprehensible, drunken lecture about his past relationship problems with a girl (who for Bret's safety will remain unnamed) and how much he cared about me and didn't want me to go down the same road with Beth.

All of this chaos resulted in a three-way fight going on at the bar with me, Bret and Beth (now on speaker phone) all yelling at each other. I got so mad that I slammed the phone down on the bar so hard that I broke it. Then I stormed out amidst a torrent of cursing. I was cursing at Beth and Bret, Bret was cursing at Beth and me and the bartender was cursing at all of us.

I was so drunk and angry that I managed to forget my coat and keys. I left them on the bar next to the broken phone. I walked over a mile to my apartment, only to realize when I got there that I couldn't get in. It was now one o'clock in the morning and my only option was to turn around and begin the long, drunken stumble back to the bar to get my keys so that I could get into my apartment.

Meanwhile at the bar, Bret and his friends had decided it was time to go home and, being helpful drunks, they picked up my jacket and keys with the hopes of returning them to me in the morning.

Around 1:30 AM, I made it back to the bar and attempted to ask if my jacket and keys were there. By this time, I was so drunk and cold that I could barely talk without concentrating very hard. Even then, I sounded like a three-year-old with a golf ball in his mouth.

The bartender, who was not at all happy to see me again, told me that my friends had taken my stuff home. So, I turned around and stumbled all the way back to my apartment, stopping only twice to relieve myself on the sidewalk.

While on the way, I somehow managed to forget all the events of the night, including the fact that I didn't have my keys to get in. Upon arriving, I searched for my keys and became enraged when I couldn't find them, so I tried to break the door down.

While in the process of flailing my limp, drunken body against the door to my apartment, I must have jarred something in my brain. I suddenly remembered that I had left my keys at the bar and had already made one unsuccessful pilgrimage back there in the hope of retrieving them. I thought for a moment about the best thing to do and I decided to go call Beth and have her bring her key over to let me in.

I stumbled to a pay phone and called her house, but she wouldn't talk to me (by now, it was after two o'clock in the morning). Her dad agreed to bring the key over to let me in. I thought to myself, "Hey, this is great!" Now I had a chance to explain why I had been so rude to his daughter and I could apologize to him. Then, I thought, he would go home and tell Beth what a stand-up guy I was for apologizing and everything would be fine.

He showed up about ten minutes later with the key and found me dozing at the foot of my front door. I woke up and tried to explain to him how responsible I had been because I hadn't driven home and how much I loved his daughter, the same daughter that my best friend and I had verbally assaulted on the phone just a couple hours earlier.

Of course, by now, the sounds coming out of my mouth were more like an old record being played in reverse on a turntable that was three speeds too slow. However, like all drunks, I thought I sounded as eloquent and sincere as a British stage-actor reciting a monologue from *Hamlet*.

I can only imagine what he was thinking as he stood there listening to the incomprehensible ramblings of a pathetic, drunken, tattooed sot who was soon to be his son-in-law. He pretended to listen while he unlocked the door and then he left.

I went to bed and woke up in the morning feeling as if everything was fine. I was surprised when I called Beth and she was angry with me. As she was letting me have it with a full-force verbal tirade, I wondered, "What's the big deal? I'm alive and everything is fine. I barely have a hangover!"Insane? Never!

I'm sure there are hundreds of alcoholics reading this who have had the same experience with different names and different places. The fact that this kind of thing happened regularly for years and that I viewed this behavior as normal is proof of my insanity. *Insanity, for me, was the belief that my abnormal behavior was normal and acceptable.*

Years later, I wrote a song about that night. I called the song, "Circus Drinking." I got the idea for the title and song from something Bret had said one night when we were drinking beer and telling "war" stories.

Inevitably, the story I have just told you came up and I was giving Bret a hard time about the things he had said to Beth that night. He responded to me by saying, "Give me a break, man. We drank like madmen that night. That wasn't normal drinking, that was circus drinking." In my mind, I pictured a carnival barker standing outside a tent shouting to the crowd,

"Step right up, ladies and gentlemen!
What you are about to see will shock you.
Please do not try this at home. These men
are trained professionals. Yes, folks, for

only five dollars, you can watch these men try to kill themselves with alcohol. That's right, ladies and gentlemen, moderation is not a word used in this tent, so no children allowed...."

If you are looking for a definition of insanity as it pertains to drinking, try comparing the way you behave when drinking to the way other people behave when they are sober.

The intensity with which I drank and the behavior that followed was only acceptable when I was around other alcoholics, just like the weird attractions at a circus are only acceptable *at a circus!* If you saw a midget dressed in tights and juggling fireballs while walking on a power line downtown, you would immediately recognize that something was out of place.

My behavior while drinking was characterized by actions that were unacceptable and out of place anywhere *except* around other insane alcoholics. However, I believed it was okay to behave that way. This, my friends, is insanity.

I could not view my behavior from the perspective of a social drinker or a non-drinker. To me, I was normal. I thought that everybody who drank acted that way! The realization that something was out of place in my behavior did not come until the pain of my addiction began to set in during the last couple of years that I was drinking.

After I had been sober for a few months, I began to realize just how horribly I had behaved numerous times. I was scared to death of ever having to come face-to-face with the people who had witnessed my exploits. Fortunately, I discovered that, just as God had given me what I needed to find sobriety, He would also give me what I needed to apologize when the time was right.

The good news is that my life was restored to sanity. God cared about me enough to pull me from the chaos that the disease of alcoholism created and He can do the same for you. He has given us the Twelve Steps to learn how to live sober. They are an example of a modern-day miracle. The millions of recovering alcoholics on the earth today are evidence of God's unconditional love.

No matter what you have done or where you have been, God will come into your life and bring you peace. However, His peace cannot come if you don't recognize the need for it. You have to want the drinking to end, and once God comes, you have to believe that it will end.

I admit that there were many times I could see no end to my drinking. Even during the last few years when I had days that I wanted to quit, I did not know how to stop. I tried several different things with the hope that I might be able to slow down or limit my drinking, but they were always short-lived and my drinking would always go back to its previous level.

My drinking continued to increase until the moment that I realized that I couldn't quit on my own. There was nothing I could do to stop. As a human, I was completely and utterly powerless over alcohol. I was so powerless, in fact, that I was literally insane when I drank.

Some might think that, at a moment like that, I would be scared or depressed. How often that is the case in life! We frequently realize that we can't accomplish something on our own, so we become upset. But for the alcoholic, it is the most glorious moment we could ever experience. It is the moment that we know we will be alright, because we finally realize that we don't have to do it alone.

It is God who is going to do it for and with us. Someone stronger than we are is there and He is telling us that we are so important to Him that He will help. You have no idea how good it felt to realize that I wasn't crazy and that I wasn't a failure because I couldn't quit drinking on my own. No alcoholic can!

So what is our response when that moment comes? What do we say or do when God seeks us out and we know that the time has come to quit? This is the essence of Step Two. We have to believe that the all-powerful creator of the universe is telling the truth. It is that simple. Do we believe what God tells us or not? He says we are worth it. Do we believe He is powerful enough to restore us to sanity or not? If we say yes, we are ready to move on to Step Two. If we say no, then we are essentially saying that we are stronger than the maker of the heavens and the earth.

If you complete Step One and truly believe in your heart, mind and soul that your life is unmanageable and that you are powerless, then the second step falls naturally into place. But if you are not convinced that you are powerless, then you will never believe that you need a power that is greater than you to give you the help you need. If there is no insanity, then there is no need to restore sanity.

If you are convinced that you aren't powerless, then you must believe that you are still in control. From this conclusion, you must make the case that you *choose* to do the stupid things you do when you drink. If this is you, well, good luck. You will probably end up dead or in jail.

I encourage you to choose recovery by choosing God. You are worth it. If you are ready to begin the process of restoring your sanity by ridding your life of alcohol, then now is the time to believe that a power greater than you can—and will—accomplish this.

You don't need to recite some long and flowery prayer. Your words don't have to be elegant or academic. Simply dropping to your knees and saying, "I believe," will do. If you believe, if you are willing to do whatever it takes to stop drinking and if you are willing to confess these things to God or whatever name you choose to give your Higher Power, then regaining your sanity is just around the corner. You can do it. You are worth it.

Insanity, for me, was the belief that my behavior while drinking was normal, when, in reality, it was only acceptable around other drunken lunatics.

Chapter III

Step Three: [We] made a decision to turn our will and our lives over to the care of God as we understood Him.

Alcoholics are weird creatures when it comes to the subject of trust. When we are drunk, we can be the most loyal and trusting people on the planet, especially when we want something from someone or when expressing our deepest, heartfelt love to an angry spouse. However, as soon as we have to deal with our own deep, dark secrets—well, suddenly we aren't so trusting.

Step Three teaches us that, in order to recover from an illness that is beyond our understanding, we must first learn to trust a Higher Power that is equally baffling. As strange as this may sound, there is some logic in this. If we could control our drinking, we would not need God to do it for us. If we could explain why we act the way we do when drinking, then we would not need God to come in and help us recover. But we can't!

Many alcoholics have a hard time coming to terms with this reality. They will admit that they don't understand why they can't stop drinking. They will also admit that their own behavior baffles them and is beyond their comprehension. Yet, these same alcoholics will refuse to trust God to help them, rationalizing that the idea of God doesn't make sense to them, that they don't understand God's ways, or even that they are mad at God. But if we can freely admit that we do not understand the disease of alcoholism, why is it that we feel the need to understand the cure (God) before we will trust it?

In recovery, I have to remember that trust in God is essential. If I stop relying on God for my strength and go back to relying on my own knowledge and power, then I know that my next drink isn't too far away. I can never ignore the fact that alcohol is always within reach. If I want to drink, it is there—waiting, beckoning to me. But with God on my side, I am safe. As an alcoholic, I will probably never fully understand the disease of alcoholism. I will also never understand God. What I do know, though, is that God can and will help me to recover from the disease of alcoholism.[*]

Someone reading this might be saying, "But what about me? I'm not unpredictable when I drink. I'm in control. I don't act any differently." If this is you, then you may not be ready for recovery. But before you decide this, ask yourself a few questions. Does your behavior change

---

[*] If you want to recover from drinking, it is important that you recognize alcoholism as a disease. Many people in today's society want to deny that fact. Strangely enough, when I was still drinking, I was also of the opinion that alcoholism was not a disease. I have since changed my thinking. Yet, despite all the research that proves alcoholism is a disease, many people still refuse to acknowledge it. I have had several arguments with people about this very subject and most of them have gone something like this:

> Person: Alcoholism is not a disease; it is a consequence of one's behavior. People choose to drink; therefore, if they develop alcoholism, it is a consequence of their choices.

> Me: Do you consider cancer a disease?
> Person: Yes, absolutely.
> Me: Okay. So if a person smokes and develops lung cancer, do they have a disease or a consequence?

You can see where I'm going with this. The same argument could be used for diabetes that results from eating habits. I will admit that I chose to drink. I will also admit that the choice to take the first drink was a bad one. I will even admit that I deserve to suffer the consequences for my choices. However, none of this changes the fact that alcoholism is a disease. Furthermore, it is a disease that produces some of the strangest behavior known to man! It takes normal and rational people and turns them into raving lunatics. It can literally turn one person into two different people. One is responsible and hardworking, while the other is totally unpredictable. Do not put off your own recovery because you refuse to acknowledge the simple fact that alcoholism is a disease!

when you can't have alcohol? If so, how? Are you more irritable? Do you suffer from mood swings? Are you difficult to be around when you can't drink? When you do drink, how much? For some people, just taking a look at the sheer volume of booze they are pouring down their throat could be an indication that there is a problem. Or, if you are spending significant amounts of money on large amounts of alcohol every week to feed your habit, then guess what? You have an addiction and chances are that you are an alcoholic.

Do not delude yourself into thinking that, just because you have never been in trouble with the law or lost a job over drinking, you are not an alcoholic. Don't get too smart for your own good. If alcohol is affecting you or anyone around you in a negative way, you may have a problem. I don't care how much money you make, how hard you work, what college you went to or what church you attend; nobody is immune to alcoholism.

When it finally gets a hold on you, it will win if you try to fight it by "making sense" out of it. You cannot make sense out of something as confusing as alcohol. I will probably never be able to explain the reasons behind my behavior when it comes to alcohol. I will also never be able to understand God or the reasons for His actions. But the good news is that, in order to stop drinking, we don't have to understand God. We just have to trust Him.

Trusting God was the beginning of my spiritual journey, and being a spiritual person is one of the main pillars of recovery. If you think you can recover from alcoholism without some kind of a spiritual element, you are wrong. To be fair, I have met a couple of alcoholics who are self-professed atheists and, through a rigorous system of positive reinforcement and behavior modification, they have been able to stop drinking and to remain sober. However, they still attend Twelve Step meetings and they also take part in service to others as part of their recovery.

In my opinion, attending meetings and looking for ways to help others denotes at least a basic spiritual understanding or commitment. I am not questioning the sincerity of these people's recovery. However, I would submit to them that they do have a spiritual element to their program, whether they recognize it or not.

I, for one, do not have the discipline required to abstain from drinking on my own. I need to have help. Help, for me, comes from God. I never have and never will understand God, but I am learning a little bit more about Him every day, and although I don't understand Him, I know He loves me (sober or drunk) and that I matter to Him. I am reminded of a quote I have heard many times; I'm not sure who said it originally, but it puts into perspective my total understanding of God.

"This I know: There is a God and I'm not Him."

I am not God. As a human alcoholic, I am not powerful enough to conquer this confusing disease, but God is! However, God could never have begun to help me to recover had I not trusted Him to do so. That is precisely what I agreed to do when I began Step Three.

As a drunk, I trusted all kinds of people with my life. I would jump into a car without thinking twice about how much the driver had drunk that night. I didn't care, as long as we were on the way to a place where there would be more alcohol. I can't even begin to count how many times I drove home after playing a gig in a bar and drinking for five, six, seven or even eight hours straight. I trusted myself to get behind the wheel or I trusted others who were inebriated to drive me home. I trusted my wife not to call the cops. I trusted my friends to forgive me for being a drunken asshole the night before. I trusted all kinds of people—so why was it so hard to trust God?

Even in high school, I trusted my friends when we were out raising hell. I remember throwing a huge party at my house one summer night when my parents were out of town. By eleven o'clock, I could barely see, so I told one of my friends (who was also drunk and completely out of control) that he was in charge of the house and I passed out. Thankfully, nothing happened, but could you imagine how that conversation with my parents would have gone? "Gee, I'm sorry, Mom and Dad. I didn't mean to burn the house down, but it wasn't my fault. You see, I drank too much, so I left one of my friends in charge of your house. So, really, it's his fault."

It comes down to this: Alcoholics don't have a problem trusting; they just have a problem trusting the right people for the right reasons. We trust other drunks with our very lives when they get behind the wheel of a car without giving it a second thought, but when we send someone for more beer, we spend ten minutes scrutinizing the receipt. We also count the change that they bring back to make sure that they didn't cheat us.

We trust people not to tell our wives or girlfriends that we were fooling around with other girls at the bar when we were out drinking. However, when we go to a barbeque, we count our beers and watch these same friends like hawks to make sure they aren't digging into our supply. How sick is all of this?

I remember one night in the fall of 1999 when my band was playing at one of the nightclubs in my hometown. Several months earlier, we had started a tradition of doing a toast with the whole bar at the beginning of the third set, around eleven o'clock. As time went on, it came to be something that we did before every set. This eventually progressed to twice a set and, finally, every couple of songs.

On that particular night, we had been drinking beer since about three o'clock that afternoon as we usually did. This was followed by the consumption of beer and shots from nine o'clock on. By the end of the night, I was so drunk I could barely breathe, let alone walk or drive. As we finished the last song, the guitar player (who was as hammered as I was) turned to me and said, "Dude, where do I live?" He was TOTALLY SERIOUS! He could not remember where he lived. So, being the helpful drunk that I was, I decided that he needed my assistance.

Did I stop him from driving? Did I call a cab? Did I call his wife to come get him? No. Instead, I DREW HIM A MAP ON A COCKTAIL NAPKIN WITH DIRECTIONS FROM THE BAR TO HIS HOUSE. I remember watching him drive away with his dome light on while trying to hold the napkin propped up against the steering wheel between his two thumbs. He was driving with his nose about five inches away from the napkin, doing his best to concentrate on the map and drive at the same time.

Isn't it amazing that, as alcoholics, we will put our trust in another drunk, or on a map on a cocktail napkin, but not the creator of the universe?

For me to get sober and to recover from my alcoholism, I knew I had to trust God. I knew that this was the only way. But what does it mean to really trust God? Basically, it means admitting that you are totally dependent upon Him.

After I quit drinking, I started to meet with a spiritual advisor. I did this for a couple of reasons. First, I recognized that my alcoholism had made me spiritually sick and, since I was working as a full-time youth minister who was responsible for forming the spiritual lives of teenagers, I felt that I should have some direction from a member of the clergy of my own faith. Second, I wanted to apply the Twelve Steps to my faith and I felt that having an older, experienced and slightly gruff priest as a spiritual "counselor" would help me to accomplish this. As it turns out, I was right about this and I'm glad I did it. The man I chose for my spiritual advisor was a Benedictine monk named Fr. Simon.

During my first session with Fr. Simon, he gave me an assignment. He told me to read the eight Beatitudes from Jesus' Sermon on the Mount in the Book of Matthew, and then to figure out why Jesus taught them in that specific order. Fr. Simon told me that he would not meet with me again until I had completed this assignment. As I listened to him give me this "homework," I thought to myself, "Well, shit, isn't that convenient! This is just like the teacher who doesn't want to deal with his students, so he gives an impossible assignment that can never be completed." What a bunch of crap, giving ME homework! Who did he think he was talking to? I was an adult!!!

These thoughts and others rumbled around in my head as I drove home. It was later that night while I was saying my evening prayers when I realized how childish my thinking had been. I had gone to Fr. Simon for spiritual guidance and help. As a recovering alcoholic, I had to be willing to do anything necessary in order to recover from my drinking. Yet, as soon as someone gave me a task that caused me to do some work, I got pissed off and oppositional. Clearly, I had some improvements to make.

For the next week, I read the Beatitudes from the fifth chapter of Matthew over and over and over again as I tried to figure out the reason behind the order in which Jesus taught them. They began to get stuck in my head as I meditated on the meaning behind the words.

1.   Blessed are the poor in spirit, for theirs is the kingdom of Heaven.

2.   Blessed are they who mourn, for they will be comforted.

3.   Blessed are the meek, for they will inherit the land.

4.   Blessed are they who hunger and thirst for righteousness, for they will be satisfied.

5.   Blessed are the merciful, for they will be shown mercy.

6.   Blessed are the clean of heart, for they will see God.

7.   Blessed are the peacemakers, for they will be called children of God.

8.   Blessed are they who are persecuted for the sake of righteousness, for theirs is the kingdom of Heaven.

The more I read them, the more it became clear to me that there were many similarities between the Beatitudes and the Twelve Steps of recovery from the AA meetings. The first thing I noticed is that the first four Beatitudes are states of being, not actions.

When I initially realized this, I was confused. How can I BE a certain way if I have never BEEN that way before? When the answer came, I got the chills. I had to let God make me that way. Only then would I be in a position to *do* the other four Beatitudes.

This is exactly the way the Twelve Steps of recovery are set up. For example, the first Beatitude reads, "Blessed are the poor in spirit, for theirs is the kingdom of Heaven." "Poor in spirit" means, "humble and lowly," and being "poor in spirit" means that you recognize your complete dependence on God for all things.

Is anyone more humble and lowly than the alcoholic who finally realizes that he cannot conquer this disease on his own? Are not the first three steps of AA the *same as the first Beatitude*? I had admitted I was powerless over alcohol and that my life was unmanageable. I believed that only a power greater than myself could restore me to sanity. Logically, the next step was to turn my will over to that power, to *trust* that power and to recognize my *dependence* upon that power!

Some may say that this sounds like a crutch. Some might accuse me of being a slave to religion. But I must confess that I found it *extremely liberating*! I was free from the shackles of alcohol and I was no longer a slave to my addiction. I finally realized that we are all slaves to something. I could either be free from my addiction and a slave to God or I could be a slave to my addiction and free of God. But I *could not have it both ways.*

Once I recognized the importance and magnitude of this reality, I had no problem understanding why the first three steps of recovery are *first* and why Jesus gave this teaching as the first of the eight Beatitudes.

Before you can recover from alcoholism, you must recognize your need for God or a Higher Power and then be willing to trust that power. You must *fully depend* upon your Higher Power. This part of your recovery has to happen before anything else can. If you are ready to trust the creator of the universe to help you with your alcoholism, all you have to do is to say a short prayer, like the following example:

God (Higher Power, etc.), I believe in You and I know that You have the power to free me from my addiction. I would rather be dependent upon You than to be a slave to alcohol. I trust You. My life is now Yours to do with as You will. Free me from this addiction and give me the strength to follow the steps of recovery so that I might choose to follow You all the days of my life.

If you just said this prayer and if you have finally decided that being a slave to God is better than being a slave to addiction, then I congratulate you. There is still a lot of hard work ahead, but you no longer have to depend on alcohol to carry you through. You now have a power much greater than booze on your side. You have the creator of the universe to walk beside you. Strangely enough, God has *always* been there, but now you really *know* it. You won't believe the difference that makes! You are worth it!

The good news is that I don't have to understand God; I just have to trust Him.

Chapter IV

Step Four: [We] made a searching and fearless moral inventory of ourselves.

God came to me and saved my life because I am worth it. But one of the harshest realities that I had to come to terms with as an alcoholic was that my recovery from alcoholism was completely contingent upon my willingness to cooperate with God.

I have heard this expressed, "God helps those who help themselves." Many people wrongfully interpret this to mean that God waits for you to do something before He will help. They falsely believe that God will only help you if you act first, drawing only on your own strength as a person. But if God only helps us after we help ourselves, then why do we need God at all?

If we are strong enough to overcome our addiction without God, then why don't we? If we have to help ourselves first, then what is the point of even believing? For me, and for so many others before me, it took help from God not only to overcome my alcoholism, but to even want to overcome it in the first place.

On the flipside of the coin, you have those who mistakenly believe that if you have enough faith, God will just come and fix you without any effort on your part. This, too, is an inaccurate way of looking at God. I personally believe that the reality is actually somewhere in the middle. I know that I can do all things because of God. He won't just do them for me, but I can't do them by myself either. I have to *cooperate* with God.

God made me aware of how important I was to Him and this gave me the courage to confront my addiction, knowing that I mattered. Once I realized this, I became willing to do anything necessary in order to end my drinking. Once I *committed* to go to any length to recover, God was there to give me the strength I needed. God gave me the courage to begin my journey to recovery, and He continues to give me strength as I grow in my spirituality. However, he doesn't just do the work *for* me. That is up to me.

Before you begin Step Four, remember that God will give you the strength and courage that is required for your recovery, but *you* must do the work. This, of course, is not always easy. In fact, it is often extremely painful.

Nothing in my life that I had ever experienced was as painful as working on Step Four. When I took an honest look at myself for the first time and wasn't able to run to alcohol for comfort, I felt worse than I had ever felt in my life. I literally had to mourn the loss of many things in my life. I had lost friendships and had missed opportunities. I had hurt others and I had hurt myself. In the course of my addiction, I had also lost the respect of many people (including myself).

At the same time I lost a certain amount of innocence. I had seen Hell and it is hard to be joyful when you live in a secret Hell created by your addiction. As my sobriety became a reality, I was forced to take a close look at myself and I was disgusted at what I saw.

I know that some may be reading this and thinking to themselves, "Why in the world would I want to quit drinking if I'm going to feel worse as a result?" To those who feel that way, I can only say that all recovery involves pain. Think of the person who is injured and must go through physical therapy in order to recover from an injury: The pain at times seems unbearable, but he faces it with courage and determination because his eyes are set on the goal of one day being restored to full health.

To complete Step Four, you must learn to approach it in the same way. Keep your heart focused on what the result will be and you will be able to deal with the pain of the obstacles along the way.

I remember a quote I once read that describes the reality of Step Four very well.

"The worst pains in the world are not physical."

I'm not sure who said this, but it is true. Rehabilitation of the soul is much more painful than rehabilitation of a torn ligament. Recovering alcoholics are some of the bravest and most courageous people in the world. In fact, many alcoholics who fail to recover do so simply because they lack faith, courage or both. The successful completion of Step Four requires one to possess both faith and courage.

Very few people have the strength to make a fearless moral inventory of their soul. It is scary and it is uncomfortable. Nobody likes to expose his or her weaknesses or secrets. For alcoholics, this is uncharted territory. Being honest with myself about my character flaws was something I had never done before. But in order to quit drinking, I had to learn how to evaluate my actions and the intentions behind them.

Before I could learn to change the way I acted, I would have to take an exhaustive moral inventory of my life. I would have to look at every detail of my character and personality and decide what was good and what was bad. I would relive many of the events from my past and decide, through prayer and discussions with my sponsor and spiritual advisor, what *was* my fault, and what *wasn't*.

I would examine my emotions, decisions and actions with what amounted to a magnifying glass for the soul in order to decide what to keep in my heart and mind and what to throw out. All of these things had to be done if I ever hoped to find peace and freedom from alcohol. But how could I possibly do this? Where was I to begin?

Previously, I mentioned the Beatitudes from the Gospel of Matthew. I presented the idea that the first three steps of recovery are basically the same as the first Beatitude. Consider the following:

1. We admitted we were powerless over alcohol, that our lives had become unmanageable.
2. We came to believe that a power greater than ourselves could restore us to sanity;
3. Made a decision to turn our will and our lives over to the care of God as we understood Him.

Each of these first three steps is summed up in Jesus' first Beatitude in the Sermon on the Mount:

"Blessed are the poor in spirit, for theirs is the Kingdom of Heaven."

Whether or not you recognize Jesus as your Higher Power doesn't matter, because the truths found in these famous teachings given by Christ transcend time and all belief systems. The parallels between the Sermon on the Mount and the Twelve Steps of recovery are fascinating. When you progress to Step Four in recovery, you are also continuing on your journey through the Sermon on the Mount. And as you work through the fourth step, you are also allowing God to mold you into conformity with the next three beatitudes."

For example, the second of Jesus' Beatitudes in the Sermon on the Mount reads:

"Blessed are they who mourn, for they will be comforted."

In Step Four, are we not mourning the loss of things? When I began Step Four, I also started the mourning process. I felt extreme sorrow and regret for my past actions. I knew I had caused harm to many (including myself) and this was extremely painful to me. I could not numb this pain with alcohol. There could be no escape through intoxication. The pain and sorrow were very real. I was the cause and I had to deal with it.

The third Beatitude from the Sermon on the Mount reads, "Blessed are the meek, for they shall inherit the land." It seems silly to have to explain why this fits so well with the fourth step of recovery, but because we are alcoholics, sometimes we need people to explain even the simplest things.

To be "meek" means to be gentle, patient, humble and mild. In many ways, this means that we must become like children. You must be as humble and as honest as an innocent child if you hope to successfully complete a moral inventory of yourself. If you lack the capacity to be humble and honest, your moral inventory will be incomplete.

As an alcoholic attempting to recover, I had to stop blaming other people. I had to accept full responsibility for my own addiction. My alcoholism was nobody's fault but my own—period! I had to accept responsibility for everything about myself. Recovery is not about pointing fingers at others. When in recovery, you must be humble enough to point the finger squarely at yourself. Recovery is about honesty and accountability. The buck stops with YOU!

Many alcoholics go through life with the erroneous belief that they are normal and that everyone else is crazy. I was especially guilty of this prior to recovering. I was a master at pointing out what was wrong with everyone else. I could always find someone or something to blame when things went wrong in order to draw the focus away from my mistakes.

I never considered for a moment that the real problem might be me. Even during my drinking days, I remember thinking to myself, "Wow, I'm glad I'm not like all those drunks in AA!" How humbling it was to finally admit that I was the problem and that I alone was responsible for my successes and my failures! I was "one of those drunks." I finally admitted that I couldn't change others, but I could change myself. I finally knew humility because, with God's help, I was able to empty myself of pride.

To be successful at Step Four, you must empty yourself of pride. This step is not about other people. It is about you. In fact, all twelve of the steps of recovery and all eight Beatitudes are about you. The only time you focus on other people during recovery is when *you apologize for what you did to them!* If you find yourself blaming others, YOU ARE NOT RECOVERING!!

Recovery is exclusively about *your* problems and *your* character flaws, not the problems and character flaws of others!!! If you refuse to let go of your pride, you will not recover from alcoholism. Furthermore, you will lack the necessary courage and faith.

Courage is probably one of the most misunderstood words I have ever come across. Many people like to believe that they are brave and courageous, but courage cannot come without fear. Courage also cannot exist in someone who is prideful. Keep in mind that there is a difference between being "proud" and being "prideful." It is okay to be proud: I am proud of my accomplishments in recovery; I am proud to be a Catholic; I am proud of the youth I work with; I am proud of my work ethic. There are many things I am proud of in others and myself.

However, being prideful is different. "Prideful" describes someone who puts himself above others, someone who believes that he is better than others on a fundamental level. Prideful people are judgmental and they create standards for others that even they cannot live up to. Prideful people don't address their own weaknesses, but are quick to tear others down for theirs.

Prideful people enjoy watching others fail because it makes them feel better. Prideful people are harsh and unrelenting in their scrutiny of those around them. Prideful people are incapable of true faith in a Higher Power because they are their own gods. Sincere belief in a Higher Power requires humility. Prideful people believe that they cannot experience fear and they interpret this to mean that they are courageous. It is important to remember that courage cannot come without fear. You have courage when you are afraid to act, but you act anyway.

As you work through Step Four, be proud of yourself for being courageous enough to admit that you are human. This may be new to many of you; it certainly was for me! Throughout my life, I set unrealistic standards for myself and when I failed to live up to them, I beat myself up further. The great thing about alcohol for me was that it numbed my feelings of inadequacy. Whenever I failed to live up to my own unrealistic standards, I would drink and, suddenly, everything felt alright again. In fact, when I was drinking, I felt as if I could accomplish just about anything.

Alcohol has been referred to many times as "liquid courage" and it was no wonder for me. When I was drunk, I believed myself to be the best at everything (including the 100-meter naked sprint). Never mind the fact that I also turned into a conceited asshole that was often completely unpredictable!

This was especially true during the years that I played music in bars while drinking heavily. I remember the last weekend that I played music with my band before ending up in a hospital for a week. This, of course, was a result of my drinking.

It was during the spring of 2000. I had taken the week off from work because we had played an out-of-town gig Thursday night. On Friday night, we had to play another gig back in our hometown. I wanted to be able to really make a binge out of the whole affair and having to go to work that week would only get in the way.

I started drinking early Wednesday afternoon and continued until sometime early Sunday morning. By Saturday night, I was a mess. Over that four-day period, I went into several walking blackouts during which I did things that I still don't remember. Some of the things that I do not remember myself remain vivid in the memories of my friends. These include my attempting to start a fight with an entire bar, getting naked and cannon-balling into a hot tub at a party, and trying to see how fast I could drive through town while turning corners without taking my foot off the accelerator.

I apparently did the last one with a car full of drunk and/or stoned friends who have since told me that they were absolutely terrified. They were literally "scared sober." I must have been pretty bad, because it takes quite a bit to terrify a carload of potheads who are stoned out of their gourd.

One of the things that I do remember was waking up Sunday morning about 3:00 AM, realizing that I was naked and in a strange home. I was on the floor of what appeared to be a kid's bedroom, although no kids were in the house. I got up and pulled a blanket around my waist and walked into the hall.

The first person I saw was Jeremy, the keyboard player from our band. He was smoking a pipe full of weed and broke into a laugh as I walked out. I asked him, "What the hell is going on?" and "Where am I?" He just continued laughing and said, "It's all good." As I stood there naked in this strange house and looked around at all the empty beer cans, the thought that came into my mind was, "No, Jeremy, it is most definitely *NOT* 'all good'."

I walked out to the hot tub where everyone else was still drinking and picked up my clothes and put them on. When Jeremy finished his pipe, I asked him to take me home. At first, he didn't want to because his "girlfriend" for the night was waiting for him, but he finally agreed. He drove me home and I stumbled into the house and fell into bed next to my wife. A few hours later, I woke up and called in sick to work. Then I checked myself into a rehab/mental health center.

This was my own decision, although I had some help from some of my drinking buddies, including Bret (Chapter I), who felt I was "a little out of control." How ironic that my drinking buddies were the voice of reason!

I spent a week in the hospital getting stabilized on some meds and, of course, avoiding alcohol. During this time, I suspected that my wife was about ready to leave me and that I had to make some changes. When she came to visit me in the rehab center, I told her that I knew she was fed up and, if she wanted a divorce, then that was fine.

However, I asked her to please wait until I got out of the hospital. I have never forgotten how my wife responded. She looked at me with a firm expression that I have only seen from her a few times in our marriage and said, "Divorce is not a word in my vocabulary." I'm so glad that my wife was so much stronger than I. For some crazy reason, she chose to stick with me. To this day, I still don't know why, but I am glad she did.

It was also during this week that I had my first real experience with the way God works through other people. You may remember that I mentioned Fr. Juan earlier. He came to see me every single morning during that week. He had such a strong impact on me that I quit playing music in bars for a long time. I even quit drinking for a couple of months. Eventually, as in the past, I returned to "the bottle" and stayed with it for another five years.

Behold, the power of alcohol! Not even a weekend like the one I had just experienced, with the possibility of losing my wife or with the influence of one of the holiest men I had ever met, could stop me from drinking. Obviously, when left to my own devices, my conduct was selfish, destructive and juvenile. Nothing good can come from such behavior.

To successfully recover from alcohol, your behavior must change. To change your behavior, you must first change the way you think. You have to align your way of thinking with God's way of thinking. If you can put your will in line with God's will, then your conduct will follow suit. Ultimately, what you want for your life must match up with what God wants for your life. This is one definition of righteousness. Another way to define righteousness is "moral conduct in conformity with God's will."

At one time or another, all of us face what appears to be an insurmountable task. Sometimes we feel like quitting even before we begin because we don't know which direction to go. However, once we start chipping away at the task, we immediately start feeling better.

Step Four is about figuring out where to start our recovery by figuring out what went wrong in the first place. If we recognize and take responsibility for our past mistakes, then it becomes much easier to change our behavior so that we can avoid those mistakes in the future. By taking a "fearless moral inventory," we are able to start exercising our moral conduct "in conformity with God's will" and to keep it there.

This step was extremely hard for me. I felt, as many alcoholics feel, that there was no place to even begin to tackle this inventory. I had made so many mistakes that, at one point, I jokingly said to a priest, "Can't you just give me some sort of general absolution so that I don't have to go through the process of dissecting my character?" His response was a resounding, "NO!" And I knew he was right. If I was serious about my recovery, I was going to have to face some pain. I was going to have to experience the refining fire that separates the gold from the dross.

All forms of purification require some pain and suffering. As I mentioned before, the worst pains in the world are not physical and, having completed this step myself as part of my own recovery, I can honestly say that the worst pains in the world for me are spiritual.

However, today I am a much more courageous person than I was before. I am at peace with God and with myself because I was willing to work through the pain in order to achieve my goal. My soul is intact and it grows stronger each day that I am willing to continue on my journey toward God. I wouldn't trade the feeling of peace that comes as a result of this work for anything in the world. You can have this feeling, too, and you will if you have the courage to stick with your recovery.

The fourth Beatitude reads, "Blessed are they who hunger and thirst for righteousness, for they will be satisfied."

If you really *thirst* for recovery and you want it badly enough, trust your Higher Power and start taking that personal moral inventory. There are many alcoholics across the world praying for you, including me. Don't wait another day. Find a quiet place and sit down with a notebook and some paper and begin Step Four.

My recovery from alcoholism was completely contingent upon my willingness to cooperate with God.

Chapter V

Step Five: [We] admitted to God, to ourselves, and to another human being the exact nature of our wrongs.

[I am going to talk a lot about my dad in this chapter and I want to stress that I do not believe that my dad is a bad guy. Dad, if you are reading this, some of this is going to hurt. I just ask that you read to the end of the chapter before forming your opinion. My dad has many good qualities and is well-respected by many people. He has come to my rescue on several occasions and I truly believe that he loves me and cares about me. There are many good things that I have learned from my dad, including how to work hard, the importance of school, time management and the importance of work before play. However, I have also had a lot of issues with my dad about the way he treated me and my family in the past. Today, I still see my dad from time to time and I do not hate him; I love him, but I believe he is sick. I believe that he is an alcoholic and has many issues that he needs to deal with if he ever wants to have a healthy relationship with my siblings. The purpose of this chapter is not to attack or blame my dad for my drinking or my problems; although the reality is that his behavior was very hurtful to me at many times and affected me in ways that contributed to my drinking. Maybe this book can be the spark that causes some honest dialogue between my father and me. I pray that this would be the case. Nonetheless, regardless of whether or not my dad and I ever talk about our history, I believe that writing about some of my experiences with my dad will help you, the reader. It is my hope that you will gain an understanding of who I am and where I come from. I am also certain that many other alcoholics have had similar experiences with a parent.]

One of the most liberating things about my recovery from alcohol is being able to admit my mistakes and take responsibility for them. I can't speak for all alcoholics, but during my drinking days, I never admitted when I was wrong. Part of my refusal to admit my mistakes sprang from the nature of my alcoholism, although part of this was also due to the way that I was raised. I grew up with a very critical father who never admitted when he was wrong. In fact, for as long as I have known my dad, I still have never heard him admit that he was wrong about anything.

Growing up in my home, I learned very quickly how to blame others or circumstances in an attempt to escape responsibility for my actions. Without question, this was something that I learned from my relationship with my dad. I was not able to admit when I had done something wrong or had made a mistake.

When I began drinking on a regular basis at the age of fifteen, this character flaw became a huge part of who I was. To quote my friends, I was always "completely full of shit." Sometimes, this was helpful to me in gaining friends. I could take any story and embellish it with half-truths, lies and exaggerations and instantly become the life of the party. I was a perfectly stereotypical "class clown." People loved to listen to me talk and tell stories. I was a great public speaker and could get just about any group of people to laugh and have a good time.

However, at other times, this was a dangerous quality that burned bridges and got me into trouble with friends, particularly when I would lie in order to avoid conflicts or trouble. In fact, most of my life was spent making excuses, lying or blaming others. By doing this, I not only taught myself to be dishonest, but I also robbed others of the opportunity to forgive me or help me. I was so focused on escaping blame that I denied myself the opportunity to grow and learn from the normal mistakes that *everyone* makes.

I conditioned myself to live life as an irresponsible teenager until the day that I woke up and realized that I was actually a thirty-year-old adolescent. I was a "grown-up," but I had never actually grown up. I had learned, through my drinking, how to avoid taking responsibility for anything. I simply refused to admit when I had made a mistake.

In my home, everyone was afraid to admit they had done anything right or wrong. We never knew what my dad's reaction would be. If we were asked a question that began with the words "Did you...," we just automatically said "no" for our own protection. It could have been a question as simple and non-threatening as, "Did you put the mayonnaise on the second shelf of the fridge?" And if we said "yes," we could very well find ourselves getting screamed at and told we were stupid.

It was not safe to make mistakes in my house and Dad always had to be right. Nobody was ever allowed to argue or disagree with Dad. His word was always first and final. There was no discussion allowed over Dad's decisions, no matter how unreasonable they were. All of us (Mom included) walked around in a state of constant fear and tension, wondering when the next explosion would occur.

Often, my dad's outbursts were over something as ridiculous as the way things were put back into the refrigerator, or whether or not you remembered to wipe off the shower door when you were finished bathing. One of the worst parts about all of this was how inconsistent my dad was. We never knew from day to day what was okay to do and what wasn't okay.

What was acceptable on Monday could trigger an explosion from Dad on Tuesday. It was just crazy! And, to make matters worse, whenever we did something that was wrong in Dad's world, not only did we get chewed out for what we had just done, but we were also reminded of every mistake that we had ever made, all the way back to birth. To survive in my house, we learned quickly to admit nothing and deny everything.

I can't speak for my brothers and sisters, but I was always afraid of Dad. He was completely unpredictable in his reactions. If ever there was a perfect example of "the alcoholic family," it was ours. Sometimes my dad's drinking made things better and put him in a good mood. There were other times when it made things much worse. He never hit us, but to be honest, I would rather have been hit than to have my dad belittle me and yell at me the way that he often did.

He would make fun of me in front of his friends or even my friends. He would poke fun at my weaknesses and he would point out my failures. He would set standards for me that I felt were impossible to live up to. He would publicly ridicule me and other family members (including my mom) in the company of complete strangers. Only five minutes later, he'd act like everything was fine. He would also get his feelings hurt if you didn't give him affection when he felt he deserved it. However, I don't remember my dad ever showing affection for me in a way that I believed to be sincere.

I remember being in the fifth grade and I was sitting outside, talking with my mom in the garage about Dad. My mom was crying as she asked me what I thought she should do about Dad. I remember having encouraged my mom to divorce him when I was only eleven years old. I remember crying along with my mom because I felt bad for her, although I didn't know what to do.

When I discovered alcohol, one of the most exciting things about it was that when I was drinking, I could escape the frustration caused by my dad's behavior. I had no idea at the time that, one day, I would grow to become an adult alcoholic that acted the same as he did. In fact, many of my character flaws are things that my dad used to do that I hated.

Every alcoholic remembers taking the first drink. As a child, there were several times that I had tasted alcohol.

When I was in the sixth grade, I started sneaking beer from our fridge and drinking it in the backyard where no one could see. I liked the taste of beer the very first time I tried it and I always wanted more.

However, what I consider to be my first real drink was when I was a freshman in high school. I got drunk with some friends while my parents were out of town. It was awesome and I loved how it made me feel! I didn't care about anything and I felt great!

By the end of my sophomore year, I was getting drunk whenever I got the chance. By the summer before my junior year, I was drinking every weekend. During my junior year of high school, I drank on most weekends and often during the week as well. That was also the year that I started drinking in the morning to get rid of hangovers. I always had a couple beers hidden in a cooler that was in my closet or in the snow outside my window.

Like most alcoholics, the drinking started slowly and increased over time. With the increase in drinking that occurred during my teenage years, I was able to turn my ability to make excuses and tell lies into an art form. As a teenage alcoholic, I had to be able to hide my drinking and partying lifestyle from my parents, my coaches and other adults.

Of course, being a good liar was not without its benefits. As I already mentioned, I could instantly become the life of the party because of my story-telling ability and charismatic personality. However, I also cultivated a certain amount of unhealthy "charm" by behaving this way. In fact, I even earned myself the nickname "Eddie Haskell" from some of my closer friends because of my ability to bullshit my way out of just about any situation. And, believe me, I could and did bullshit myself out of just about everything.

I remember one of the many nights I came home drunk. I was sixteen and had downed an entire bottle of whiskey in less than four hours (which could have very easily killed me at that age). I told my mom that I was going to the movies, but had gone to my friend Angus's house instead (my friends and I spent a lot of time at Angus's house because his dad would buy us booze and let us party in his basement). Angus and I both wanted to go into the military when we got out of high school. I wanted to go into the Marines and Angus wanted to enlist in the Army.

From the spring of my sophomore year of high school to the summer of my senior year, I drank A LOT of booze in Angus's basement.

That particular night, after I finished the bottle of whiskey, I drove home and walked into our living room at about 12:30 AM. I could barely stand up and I had dried puke all over the front of my shirt. My mom had been dozing on the couch with the lights off. I think the fact that it was dark in the room is what saved me (not to mention that my mom was half asleep). She asked about the movie and I told her, "It was great." I proceeded to tell her all about it (I had read a review of it in the newspaper earlier that day so that I would have a solid alibi).

After having listened to me explain the plot of the movie, she asked why I had been gone for five hours if the movie was only two hours long. I spent the next twenty minutes telling her a creative lie that covered all of the important angles. I explained how my date and I had gone to the movie and, once there, we ran into some other friends who wanted to go get a hamburger when the movie was over.

I told her that we went across the parking lot to the bowling alley to eat and ended up staying to bowl a few games, explaining that was why I smelled like smoke (it certainly wasn't because I had chain-smoked cigarettes since leaving the house five hours ago).

After we had finished bowling, I explained, we decided to go get an ice cream sundae at an all-night restaurant. Unfortunately, the restaurant was also a favorite hangout for drunks coming home from the bars and, while we were walking out of the restaurant, a drunken guy standing by his truck started yelling at us and tried to start a fight. During the scuffle, he ended up puking all over me (which is why I smelled like puke and whiskey). "That made me so mad," I told my mom. I even added, "Drunk people are so stupid!"

Then I told her that the restaurant owner had to call the police and we all had to stay until the police arrived so that we could fill out the police report and be responsible citizens. That, of course, is why I ended up getting home so late.

Upon finishing the story, I headed toward my room and promptly fell down the stairs. "Whoops! Sorry, Mom, I just slipped. I guess I'm still a little shaken up. I'm okay though. Goodnight!"

These are the kind of stories that I told practically every weekend throughout high school. They were always different, but never too extraordinary, at least in my mind, anyway, so they were believable. Of course, I don't believe for a minute that my drinking went undetected throughout all of high school.

By the time I was approaching my senior year, I am positive that my parents knew that I was drinking. Although my dad didn't seem to care, I think my mom was afraid to confront me about it. I was willing to do anything or tell any lie to avoid getting caught and I'm sure my mom knew that I would deny it at any cost, so why should she even bother bringing it up?

I was also willing to do anything or tell any lie to avoid admitting a mistake in other areas, as well. I can't begin to remember how many pranks I must have pulled throughout my high school years and I was almost never caught. On the few occasions that I did get caught, I was either able to talk my way out of it or to minimize the punishment by convincing my captors (teachers, principal, coaches) that it really wasn't my fault. I claimed that I was just a victim of circumstance. This kind of behavior did not go away after high school. In fact, it became worse in some ways.

I remember one incident that happened about a year before I quit drinking. I have been involved in martial arts since I was in the fifth grade. When I got out of the Marines, I got into amateur boxing and, despite my drinking, actually did pretty well at it. I quit competing in 1998, but I still love to watch boxing and MMA (mixed martial arts) fights.

One night, my friend Terry, with whom I had played music, invited me to come to watch his girlfriend fight in an MMA "cage fight" at one of the big event centers. I was excited by the invitation and I agreed to go. The fights that night were really great and so was the booze. Before the last fight was over, I was totally smashed.

At the conclusion of the last fight, Terry and I headed to the sports bar on the second floor of the event center. We sat at an outside table on the veranda along with some other friends, including Terry's girlfriend (who had won her fight). As we continued drinking, we talked about boxing and music and, as the night progressed, I became more and more out of control.

It was during a lull in the conversation that I began throwing little things from our table over the edge of the balcony and onto the sidewalk below. I didn't even get up from the table to see where they were landing or if they were hitting anybody. I was just picking up things like matchbooks, cigarettes and ashtrays and throwing them over the edge.

Finally, I became bored with this game and decided to make it more interesting. I dared Terry to throw a 22 oz.

"schooner" sized beer-glass over the edge. He said I was crazy and he refused to do it. I kept pushing him until he finally told me, "Shut up, and do it yourself." So, I did. I just chucked the empty mug over the edge and didn't even bother to look over to see if it might have hit someone. We all laughed about it, despite the fact that someone could have been lying unconscious on the sidewalk below, with blood dripping from his or her scalp. In a few moments, we had forgotten all about it and continued drinking.

About twenty minutes later, we were at the bar, buying another pitcher of beer and a round of shots. The bartender gave us our order and, when we turned around to walk back to our table, we were confronted by a group of eight or nine very angry guys. The one in front didn't waste any time. He walked up to me, got right in my face, and asked, "Did you throw a fucking glass over the edge of the balcony?"

Despite my drunkenness, I quickly realized that this could turn out badly for both Terry and me. However, my charm had never failed me before, so I decided to do my best to talk my way out of the situation. I knew I couldn't lie and say I didn't do it, because too many people had seen me throw it over. However, I knew that, if I played my cards right, I could calm them down and maybe even make friends with them. I pretended that I didn't hear what he had said, so I asked, "What?"

As I said this, I reached behind me and picked up an empty beer bottle off of a table. I decided to give myself a little insurance in case my charm failed. I kept the bottle behind my back while I waited for the guy to ask me the question again. Out of the corner of my eye I could see that Terry was nervous and had seen me grab the bottle. The guy asked me again, "Did you throw a fucking beer glass over the balcony?"

Before I could answer, Terry tried to jump in and save me by blurting out, "You mean that went over? Whoops, I thought it just landed in the plants!" There were potted plants along the edge of the balcony. "Nice try, Terry", I thought, "but they aren't going to buy that this was an accident."

"Yes," I said, in my most charming, amiable tone, "I threw a glass over the railing. We were being stupid at our table and, obviously, we have had too much to drink. Sorry about that." I then lied and said that I had looked over the edge and hadn't seen anybody and that I had even walked down to make sure nobody was hurt.

The guys were totally stunned. They had expected a denial and an explanation, anything but a confession. However, there I was, admitting it and even sounding very sincere about my apology. Of course, in my mind, I was anything but sincere or sorry. I was thinking, "Okay, if my charm fails, I'm going to break this bottle over the first guy's head, kick the guy to my left in the crotch and, from then on, I will just take them as they come".

Luckily, the confrontation never came to blows. They just stood there and didn't know what to say. Finally, one of them asked me why I did it and told me that I deserved to "get my ass kicked." I responded in my most sincere voice that I was just "being stupid" and that he was absolutely right, I should get my ass kicked. I even offered that, if they all wanted to fight me, I would go outside and fight.

They had no idea how to respond to this and, within five minutes, they were all sitting with me drinking beer (that I had purchased) and treating me like I was their best friend. They were impressed by how "brave" I was to own up to it and apologize. But I wasn't sorry; I was just full of shit.

The funny thing is that the more they talked to me, the more they started to like me and hate Terry. They started saying stuff like, "Yeah, well, you're cool because you admitted it, but that other guy is a chicken shit. We should kick his ass!" As the night went on, they began to convince themselves that I really hadn't done anything and it had been Terry that threw the glass.

They talked themselves into believing that I was just covering for my friend. I, of course, allowed them to believe this. Naturally, I had to warn Terry to watch his back and I told him that it would probably be a good idea to get out of there as soon as he could—but, hell, I was safe!

The crazy and sick thing about this story is that it didn't happen when I was eighteen or twenty-one. It happened when I was almost thirty and was working full-time for a church as a YOUTH MINISTER!!!! Not even working for a church could cause me to change my behavior and be honest with people. I was still full of shit and, when I wanted to, I could talk my way out of anything.

Throughout my life, I had lied to my parents, teachers, principals, bosses, girlfriends, friends, brothers, sisters—you name it. I could not be wrong, EVER! I could not fail. I could not get caught. Inside, I knew that many times I was wrong. There were many times that I should have owned up to things I had done, but something always stopped me from taking the blame. So I would just stand quietly by while a friend would be punished and I would go free. I could shift blame quicker than I could tap a beer keg.

When I made mistakes, I certainly knew it on the inside and I was the first to recognize my failures. But I would never talk about them, even though I would dwell on them for years and allow them to tear my self-esteem apart. Every time I told a lie or led someone to believe that I was something I wasn't, I added one more ounce of weight to the crushing load I was already carrying on my conscience. I knew I did not measure up to the standards I had set for others, although that didn't stop me from pointing out everybody else's mistakes and failures in order to prevent anyone from seeing mine.

In Step Five of the Twelve Steps, I realized that it was finally time for me to start owning up to my mistakes. To complete this step, I had to tell God and another human being the exact nature of my wrongs. It was finally time to admit everything. I had to tell it all. I had to spill my guts.

This step reminds me of a scene from one of my favorite movies, *The Goonies*. In one scene, some bad guys capture a young boy nicknamed Chunk and tell him to "spill his guts" about a hidden treasure they're after. They demand that Chunk tell them "everything."

"Everything?" Chunk asks.

"Yes," they respond, "Everything."

Chunk interprets this to mean that they literally want to know *everything* about him and he proceeds to tell them his life story, including every bad thing he has ever done. The scene itself is hilarious. I remember watching the movie with my wife and she said, "I can't imagine sitting down and telling someone every bad thing I have ever done." Isn't it ironic that she would say that to me, an alcoholic, who has done exactly that?

Step Five is the first step that requires that you actually do something outside of yourself. You have to involve another person. Steps one through four are very internal. They are about allowing God to begin making changes inside of you. In Step Five, you step outside of yourself by bringing in another human being.

In Chapter III, I began talking about Jesus' Sermon on the Mount and the Beatitudes. I explained how the first four Beatitudes are only states of being. They are not things that you can do, but instead are ways that you are. You cannot do the first four Beatitudes. Instead you must let God do them for you and within you so that you are then prepared to do the remaining four.

The Twelve Steps of recovery work the same way. In Steps One through Four, you are allowing God to come in and change the way that you are. In Step One, I admitted that I was powerless, but only after God showed me how powerless I was. He came to me.

Secondly, I believed God when He said that I mattered to Him, but I still didn't really do anything other than agree with God. In the third step, I allowed God to take over my addiction for me. Again, God is the one working, not me. In the fourth step, I allowed God to show me the flaws in my character and in my way of living by completing a fearless moral inventory. The only thing I actually did in Step Four was write down a list of flaws that God told me I needed to fix.

But in Step Five, it was finally time for me to do something. This fits in perfectly with the fifth Beatitude, which states:

> "Blessed are the merciful, for they will be shown mercy."

In this Beatitude, Jesus tells us that, in order to be shown mercy, we must first be merciful to others. Showing mercy is something that we do. We begin living this Beatitude when we complete the Fifth Step of recovery. When we admit our faults to God and to another human being, we are opening the door to God's mercy in our lives.

Don't make the mistake of thinking that the best thing about this step is being able to get things off of your chest. Rather, the coolest thing is that we learn how to show mercy to others. I admit that being able to finally "come clean" about all your mistakes feels great. But the most important thing that I learned from this step is how to be merciful to other people.

In the Catholic Church, we have the sacrament of Reconciliation, commonly referred to as "confession." To sit down and tell somebody all that you have done wrong is a very humbling experience. Confession is very similar to the Fifth Step. By sitting down and confessing to somebody every single thing that you have done wrong, you not only feel better, but you also learn to be merciful because you get to experience someone being merciful to you!

You get to see God's mercy through the example of another human being. It is impossible to show mercy to others until you see it in action from someone else. In Step Five, you get to see someone reflect the mercy of God because they hear every bad thing about you and still love you anyway! This is truly the coolest thing about Step Five and about the fifth Beatitude.

As a Catholic, I had been to confession many times, but I never realized how much I was missing by not being totally honest about all of my problems. However, when I completed Step Five, I began to see what mercy really was for the first time in my life. I experienced my first real taste of what Jesus was really calling us to do when he said to be merciful. Being merciful is about forgiving and loving, not about judging. Judgment is for God alone.

I cannot express in words how amazing it was to be able to tell all my faults to someone and not be judged. Since completing my fifth step, I know that I have learned to show mercy to others in ways I never understood before.

When I am presented with an opportunity to be merciful, I just remember how I felt when I did the Fifth Step. I remind myself how scared and nervous I was about baring my soul to another human being. I try to remember that whoever is seeking my mercy or my forgiveness probably feels the same way I did.

When I do this, I am able to forgive much more easily, because I remember being shown mercy at a time when I desperately needed it.

The greatest blessing of Step Five is that you learn to forgive and you learn how to avoid judging people. It is the greatest feeling in the world to be able to forgive. I am able to forgive others now because I know that I am also forgiven—and I can now say that I forgive my dad.

This past year, my wife and I moved two thousand miles to a new home. It was a tough decision, but we felt it was the right one. As we got closer to the month of November, we began making plans to spend our Thanksgiving far away from our home and our family. Out of the blue, my dad called me and asked if we would like to come spend Thanksgiving with him, his girlfriend and my brothers. He offered to pay our airfare if we wanted to come.

It had been a couple years, at this point, since I had last seen my dad. When my grandfather died, I had spent about a week with Dad. Before that, the last time I had seen him had been during the previous year, when I visited my grandfather for the last time. It wasn't like I never had any contact with my dad. I just didn't see him very often. He called from time to time and always sent us money at Christmas and on birthdays, but we really didn't talk much other than that.

After talking with my wife, we decided to go out and spend Thanksgiving with him. It was the best Thanksgiving I have ever had. I got to see my brothers, whom I love dearly, and my dad was wonderful.

On the morning that we left to fly back home, my dad took us to the airport. He waited while we checked our luggage and then walked to security with us. As we waited in line, I kept looking back to see if he was still there and, each time I looked, there he was, waving goodbye.

Just like when I was seventeen and was leaving on a bus for the Marine Corps, he was there waving goodbye. Just like when I would come home on leave to visit, he would always take me to the airport and be there, waving goodbye. When I got out of the Marines, he was there to pick me up at the airport. When I married my current wife, he was there, outside the church, waving goodbye as we drove off. When I left California after my grandfather's funeral, there was Dad, waving goodbye. He wasn't perfect, but he was always there.

Eventually, I got through security at the airport that day and, as I rode up the escalator, I looked back one last time. There was dad, waving goodbye. A tear came to my eye as I waved back. I love my dad; I always have. But for the first time, I realized that he is finding his own way, just as I am finding mine.

For some of us, this happens early and for others it may be later in life. Regardless of how or when it happens, I know he will always be my dad, and I will always love him. I am now able to fully recognize his love for me because of what I have learned in my recovery during the Fifth Step.

As I did the Fifth Step, I decided to tell all of my wrongs to a priest within the sacrament of Confession. It was not an easy thing to do and, at the time, it was painful for me. Looking back on it, it was also a little funny. The priest was a good friend of mine who was aware of my alcoholism and knew that I was in recovery.

However, he really didn't know much about the disease of alcoholism or how "insane" some alcoholic behavior can be. Needless to say, I'm not so sure he was ready to hear everything that I told him, but he listened patiently while I "spilled my guts" for about two hours.

He rarely interrupted as I read from my notebook, reciting the list of things I had done and behaviors that I needed to change. I could tell a number of times that he was a little shocked as I enumerated my transgressions. His eyebrows would raise and he would get this slightly horrified expression on his face that quickly turned into a look of deep concern.

At the end of it, I certainly felt better, although I'm not so sure about him. However, he did tell me that he wanted a copy of the AA book so that he could be more informed about alcoholism in order to better minister to his parishioners. All in all, it worked out well for him and for me. I completed Step Five and, in the process, I helped to educate someone in a pastoral position about the reality of alcoholism.

If you are an alcoholic and are ready to complete Step Five, I recommend going to someone who is familiar with the disease of alcoholism so that you don't shock them too much. I suggest a pastor, a counselor or perhaps a sponsor. I strongly discourage going to a friend or a family member (for obvious reasons). However, in reality, it doesn't really matter who you go to, as long as you do it. You could even grab some stranger off the street if you wanted to. The important thing is to do it! If I can do it, anyone can.

And remember, although it may be tough and painful to do, the benefits that your heart and soul will receive from completing this step will totally outweigh the pain you will experience in the process. When you have finished, you will feel as if a huge weight has been lifted from your shoulders. You will not be able to stop smiling! Your heart, your mind and your soul will feel completely cleansed and you will know it! You will be shown mercy and, in turn, you will be able to show mercy to others. This is very important if you want to be able to complete the future steps. You can do it! You are worth it! I believe in you!

I knew I did not measure up to the standards I set for others, but that didn't stop me from pointing out everybody else's mistakes and failures in order to prevent anyone from seeing mine.

Chapter VI

*Step Six: [We] were entirely ready to have God
remove all these defects of character.*

Step Six is also a cool step in the process. No matter how painful your recovery has been up to this point, you can't help but feel excited about the prospect of the creator of the universe removing the things from your character that have caused you problems. This step seems to happen in different ways for different people. Some alcoholics claim that their lives instantly change overnight, while others (like me) report a different experience.

Completing Step Six for me was more like making a pact with God. He promised to remove my faults and I promised to practice living without them. In other words, I knew God could remove them, but that removal was contingent upon my willingness to stay in constant contact with God. As days turned into weeks and weeks into months, I became so good at *practicing* my new way of life that it actually *became* my new way of life. For me, Step Six took place over an extended period of time.

Looking back on my life during my drinking days, it makes perfect sense that I would have to practice living without my defects of character before they would cease to be a part of me. After all, I certainly did my share of "practicing" being an alcoholic. I began drinking at the age of fifteen and didn't quit until I was thirty.

This means that I spent fifteen years practicing to be the best alcoholic I could be, so why should I expect to become a changed person overnight? Alcoholism was almost like a sport for me. I practiced my alcoholism with as much intensity and devotion as that of an athlete in training.

I love boxing and, for three years, I competed in amateur boxing (Golden Gloves) tournaments, so I will use boxing as an example. Think for a moment of the professional boxer who trains every day. Boxing ceases to be a sport and becomes his way of life—a discipline. People have been killed in the boxing ring, but that doesn't deter other boxers from competing. Alcoholics die every day, but that doesn't deter others from drinking. I know this because, in high school, I had a close friend who died an alcohol-related death, and that didn't stop me from drinking.

In Chapter V, I briefly mentioned a friend named Angus. We used to party at his house nearly every weekend because his dad would buy us booze. I could tell you story after story about the crazy nights that started, and sometimes ended, in Angus's basement. Many of these stories are hilarious.

They are full of good times and laughter, along with the ever-present element of teenage rebellion. Although it sounds like the ultimate cliché, Angus's basement was a place where we truly did share our hopes and dreams. We also shared countless cases of beer and half-gallon bottles of vodka.

We were "just a bunch of drunk, crazy teens." Even after the night that Angus accidentally shot himself in the head and ended his life, we still believed we were invincible.

Angus was a good friend of mine. I had not known him nearly as long as many of the other "regulars" that frequented Angus's basement, but when we met, we instantly hit it off. We both wanted to go into the military after high school. Angus wanted to go into the Army and I wanted to go into the Marines.

Angus was a very unique character. He was Scottish and would often listen to his favorite bagpipe music when we were all drinking. His favorite song to listen to on the bagpipes was "Amazing Grace." He, like me, was also completely and totally full of shit.

When I met Angus, I realized that I had finally met someone who could make up stories that were even more outlandish than mine. Whether he was talking about the time he "shot a drug dealer in Las Vegas" or the time he was "jumping out of airplanes with the Army Rangers," you couldn't help but be drawn in by how convincing he sounded.

I think he told those stories so many times that he actually began to believe that they had really happened. To be honest, I think they would have eventually happened if he had lived to finish high school.

Angus was obsessed with his dream to go into the military. We would get drunk and sit outside his house, drinking until dawn and talking about our future military careers. Angus would smoke his non-filter cigarettes and drone on and on about all the places he would go after he enlisted in the Army.

We would argue about which branch of the military was best. Sometimes tempers would rise, but we always ended our heated discussions by professing our devout love for each other, the kind that can only come from two people who are completely intoxicated beyond all possibility of rational thought or speech.

Just about everywhere Angus went he was dressed in camouflage army fatigues. However, his outfit would not be complete without his fifteen-inch Bowie knife and his black, military 45 caliber automatic. I know that sounds crazy, but his pistol was as much a part of him as his short, red hair. In fact, when we would all get drunk and go out on the town, we used to have to fight with him to get him to leave his pistol in the truck. This would happen whether we were going to a restaurant, to the movies, into a bowling alley or anywhere else.

I can't tell you how many wrestling matches took place in various parking lots around town between Angus and all of us as we tried to take his pistol away from him before we went into a place of business. I can't imagine what people walking by must have thought. If you had been walking by on one of those nights, you would have seen three or four teenagers wrestling around with another teen (fully dressed in camouflage) and shouting random profanities intermixed with strange references to a "pistol." I am amazed that nobody ever called the police.

In the end, Angus would always finally surrender his side arm and, after safely stowing it in the glove box, we would all stumble drunkenly into wherever we were going. Just thinking back on those times as I write this, it makes me wonder how I could ever have thought that this type of behavior was normal.

Angus also owned an AR-15 rifle (the semi-automatic version of the M16) and a short-barreled, pistol-grip shotgun. He usually left the rifle and the shotgun at home, although they were always loaded and within easy reach of anyone who happened to be drinking in his basement on any given night.

As teenagers living in a rural community, we believed that nothing went together better than alcohol and firearms. When you consider all the booze, guns and cigarettes that were in Angus's basement on a typical weekend, I'm surprised that we were never raided by the ATF.

One August morning, I received a phone call that should have changed my life. A girlfriend of mine called me early on a Saturday to tell me that Angus was dead and that another friend of mine was also in the hospital. Apparently, Angus had had a party at his house and had gotten drunk, as always.

He had sat down on the floor with his back resting against a couch and began twirling his pistol around. One of the girls at the party was a sister of my friend Bret (see

Chapter I). Her name was Staci and she was worried about Angus messing around with his pistol while he was drunk. She walked over to him to ask him to be careful. Angus responded, "Don't worry, the safety is on, see?" He put the gun to his head and pulled the trigger.

The bullet went through Angus's head and into Staci's leg. Angus died instantly. Staci carried that bullet in her leg until just recently. We have all carried the pain of Angus's death with us to this day. The week before school started, instead of being out enjoying the last days of our summer freedom, we were all standing at Angus's grave as friends and pallbearers, listening to bagpipes play "Amazing Grace" while Angus's coffin was lowered into the ground. At that point in my life, I had been drinking for only three years. I went on to drink for nearly another thirteen.

The death of my friend did not cause me to see the danger of drinking. In fact, when Angus died, I didn't think for a moment that alcohol was to blame. I blamed myself for not being there to stop it. I blamed Angus for being unsafe with a firearm. I blamed God for taking Angus's life. But blame alcohol? Never! I continued to drink and fuel my addiction for many more years. I continued to practice my alcoholic way of life. Angus's death did not instantly change me, even though it should have.

It is important to remember that, when you quit drinking and enter recovery, you should not expect instant change any more than you would expect it in any other area of your life. Also you should not expect others to immediately trust you and treat you differently. Just like it took years to burn bridges and hurt others, it will take some time to repair relationships and earn back the trust of friends and family members who were caught in the path of your addiction-tornado.

It is also important to remember that relationships cannot be restored and wounds cannot be healed until *you* are healthy and on the path to serenity. *You* have to be okay before you can start rebuilding relationships and making amends for the harm you caused through your addiction.

That is why Step Six is so important. In order for me to change who I had become, I had to get rid of my "defects of character." By doing so, I could become the kind of person who could begin repairing my past. If I wanted to regain the trust of people whom I had harmed, then I needed to present them with a genuine product.

When the time came for me to stand before those who suffered because of my addiction, I had to know in my heart that I was a changed person if I expected them to believe it. My heart, mind and soul had to be intact. My intentions had to be pure. I had to be "clean of heart." This comes from the sixth Beatitude from Jesus' Sermon on the Mount:

"Blessed are the clean of heart, for they will see God."

To be "clean of heart" means to have the right motives and intentions in the things you do. Are you seeking God's glory through your actions, or are you seeking glory for yourself? Are your actions meant to lift someone up or help someone, or are your actions meant to hurt or degrade somebody? If your actions are selfish or if t hey are motivated by jealousy or anger, you are not clean of heart.

Once the first five Beatitudes are in place, only then are we able to truthfully evaluate the motivation behind the things we do. Think about that for a minute: How can you truthfully evaluate your actions and your intentions if you are missing any of the first five Beatitudes? You can't; it is impossible! We *must* have pure intentions in all that we do and seek forgiveness when we do not.

Furthermore, if our character is riddled with flaws, there is no way that we can be clean of heart. This is why

Step Six is so vital to our recovery. Our character has to be intact before we can move on to Step Seven.

I can honestly say that, when I was drinking, my intentions were not pure. As a rule, I was selfish and, more often than not, my actions were motivated by jealousy and anger. It was all about ME! This doesn't mean that I didn't care about others, because there were a lot of people that I cared about and went out of my way to help, including many of the teens I worked with. But many times, my motivation for providing help was wrong and misguided.

Sometimes, I helped so that I could look good. At other times, I helped because it made me feel better. However, the main reason I helped others was because it allowed me to ignore my own problems. By helping others, I could continue to rationalize and justify my alcoholism. I convinced myself that God would tolerate my alcoholism because I spent so much time helping teens.

I also justified my drinking by saying that it helped me deal with the stress of working with teens in stressful environments. Overall, I falsely believed that the *good things* I did for others made up for the *bad things* that resulted from my alcoholism and that my drinking was justified because of the stress of my work. Unfortunately, that is NOT how God operates.

No amount of helping teens could possibly make up for all of the harm that I had done to others and to myself while drinking, especially when I was doing good things for the wrong reasons or doing bad things (getting drunk) to bring about good things (stress relief). You can never do evil to bring about good and still be clean of heart. It is my belief that in recovery, in life and in the eyes of God, "the end never justifies the means."

If you remember anything from this chapter, remember this: If you want to see God, you must have a clean heart. This doesn't mean that to *experience* God you must have a clean heart.

I had already *experienced* God, but now, in Step Six, I was going to *see* God. By asking God to remove my defects of character, I was able to see what God did and is still doing in me. I am a walking miracle and the transformation of my character proves that miracles still can and do occur.

By completing Step Six and asking God to remove my defects of character, I was finally able to truthfully evaluate my actions. I was able to do things for the right reasons. When I had tough decisions to make, I knew how to look at the intentions of my heart and put others before me. I no longer felt bad about decisions I made.

I didn't feel like I had to do *good things* in order to make up for *bad things*. This doesn't mean that I didn't make mistakes. What it does mean is that, even when I did make mistakes, they didn't create the kind of guilt in me that they had before because I knew I had the right intentions in the things that I did. I was no longer motivated by selfishness.

My life was becoming a life that was motivated by concern for others. I was now being moved by compassion. The direction in my life became clear as I better understood the purpose of life. I ultimately came to believe that the purpose of life is to love and serve God and others.

I still believe this today, although I still have to practice. It is amazing how quickly old ways of thinking can creep back into my heart and mind if I let my guard down. My own recovery from alcoholism is a day-to-day process that I could choose to discard at any time.

It would take no effort on my part to wake up one day and decide to drink. All it would take is for me to stop caring long enough to get to the store and buy a case of beer. However, it does take effort on my part to wake up each day and decide that today I am going to take the hard road instead of the easy one.

Today, I am going to follow God's will instead of my own. Today, I am going to serve God and help others. Today is not about me. Today, I am not going to drink!!!

It takes practice to live sober, and it takes practice to live without your defects of character. As I have already stated, you must practice your new way of living until eventually it becomes a part of you. Just because God agrees to remove your character flaws, it does not mean that you won't choose to go back to them.

Every day, you must wake up and decide to live according to God's will instead of your own. Some days have been easy for me and others have been hard, but nothing worthwhile comes without effort.

As I write this, I have been sober for just over two years. I still have to evaluate my actions and decisions on a daily basis. I still have to be on my guard against old ways of thinking and being. But it is worth it because I am happy. I am happy with what God is doing in me and through me.

When I help others today, it is for the right reasons. I have firsthand experience of the miracle that God has worked in my heart and mind. I look the same, but inside I am different. My reasons for doing things are different. My reactions to problems and obstacles are different and my outlook on life is different. It is the most wonderful feeling in the world to be delivered from selfishness and to live your life looking for ways to build others up.

One of my favorite quotes about freedom is as follows:

"True freedom is not the ability to do what you want, but the ability to do what you ought."

Pope John Paul II said that. Today, I know that, for me, this quote rings true. Being clean of heart is the answer to finding and experiencing true freedom and completing Step Six is how you begin that journey. You can do it. You are worth it.

Just like it took years to burn bridges and hurt others, it will take some time to repair relationships and earn back the trust of friends and family members who were caught in the path of your addiction-tornado.

Chapter VII

Step Seven: [We] humbly asked Him to remove our shortcomings.

There is a big difference between an alcoholic who is "in recovery" and an alcoholic who just "isn't drinking." Just because you aren't drinking, it doesn't mean that you aren't still an alcoholic.

In AA meetings, you will sometimes hear people refer to a "dry drunk." This is someone who isn't currently drinking, but still displays the abnormal behavior of an alcoholic. This could even mean someone who has quit drinking but still has never recovered from alcoholism.

People in this category could spend their whole life "not drinking" but still never be truly free from the effects of alcohol. This is because the disease of alcoholism changes us to the point that we become someone different than our true self, whether we are drinking or not.

Alcohol destroys our character and it stains our soul. Our addiction to alcohol waters down the good in us and brings out the bad. It enslaves us and the chains of alcoholism cannot be broken without the help of our Higher Power. We are never free from its grasp until we are in the grip of God's steady hand.

Once God is in control instead of the alcohol, we can begin using the Twelve Steps to "reprogram" ourselves. Through these steps, we learn a new way to live. This is called "recovery." I accept the fact that I will be in recovery for the rest of my life. If I don't like being in the hands of God, I can always turn back to my old master, alcohol. I hope and pray that I never will.

I must never forget that alcohol is always there, waiting, beckoning and softly calling me back to my old way of living. The battle will never end, but if I persevere, my life will only continue to get better.

There were two times in my life that I was a "dry drunk" and, if you ask those who had to live around me, you will find that I was much harder to put up with at those times than the times when I was drinking. The reason for this is that I couldn't have my "fix." If you take a drug away from any addict, you must be prepared for the worst.

I was no exception to this rule. Almost every AA meeting that I go to, I hear someone talk about how the Twelve Steps are more about living than they are about alcohol. In so many ways, this is true. The only step that mentions alcohol is Step One. The rest of the steps are about getting your life in order so that you can live without alcohol. That is what recovery is all about: living your life without having to hide behind alcohol.

However, in order to accomplish this task, I had to actively work the 12 steps. If I could live life without alcohol, then I wouldn't need the Twelve Steps. But the reality is that I am an alcoholic and, accordingly, I must work the steps in order to live life on life's terms.

The purpose of Step Seven is to get rid of all those character flaws that led you to drink or that came about as a result of your drinking. Many of my character defects developed and became worse the more that I drank. They became especially dangerous, though, when I *wasn't* drinking.

Sometimes my drinking brought these character flaws to the surface; at other times, it would hide them. For example, my drinking would often temper my rage and my anger, while, at the same time, increase my lust or bitterness. In contrast, when I wasn't drinking, my anger and rage would become out of control.

A number of other character flaws were still evident in my life, whether I was drinking or not. For example, I was not a very honest person, regardless of whether I was drunk or sober. I often lied to avoid taking responsibility for my actions. I was also a very cynical and critical person by nature, whether drunk or sober. I had a difficult time showing compassion or kindness to others.

Many times I would hurt somebody with my words or actions and then, if I started to feel remorse or sorrow for my actions, I would simply drink until I felt better. Alcohol did a great job of numbing my conscience. I know that I hurt many people when I was drinking and I hurt them worse when I failed to apologize. If anyone was ever in need of a character "tune-up," I was that person.

In order for me to start figuring out what my character flaws were, I had to look back through my life at my behavior and determine the motivation behind the hurtful things that I had done. In some cases, I had to evaluate my life one action at a time. I had to look at what I did that was wrong and then figure out why I did it.

This was a very difficult and emotional process. It was not only hard because I had to relive some of the pain I had caused others; it was also often very hard to figure out what the specific character flaw was that led me to do hurtful things. However, I finally found a way of doing this that helped to clear things up.

I began to look at the kind of behavior that was predominant at those times in my life when I wasn't drinking. It was much easier to remember specific details about the times when I was a "dry drunk," because those memories were not clouded by the effects of alcohol. I could see very clearly what kind of person I had become by looking at how I behaved without alcohol in my system.

As I scrutinized my actions and feelings from those times and compared them with my actions while drinking, I came to realize that the *same character flaws were present in my behavior, whether I was drunk or sober.* This brought home to me the full realization of how serious the disease of alcoholism can be.

If I ever hoped to truly find freedom from alcohol, I had to ask my Higher Power to remove the defects in my character. The first part of Step Seven is to figure out what those defects are. I had to make a list. To accomplish this, I specifically examined the two periods in my life when I had stopped drinking for a significant amount of time.

The first time was during my first year in the Marine Corps. I didn't drink while I was in Boot Camp and managed to stay away from alcohol for about the next nine months. I threw myself into my religion and put on an outward appearance of being a very pious person.

It was during this nine-month period that I learned a very important lesson, even if I didn't fully understand it until now: Religion without spirituality is useless. A person can go through all kinds of motions on the outside, but if they are not spiritual on the inside, they have gained nothing and they have lost everything.

I went to church, I read Scripture and I even prayed, but I was not a spiritual person. I was still very critical of others. I developed a strong sense of self-righteousness. I based my own worth and my relationship with God on how well I was doing compared to others. I was habitually dishonest; I was a phony.

My reasons for being religious were not pure. It was all about me. I expected God to answer my prayers because of what I was doing. I thought that because I went to church and had others convinced that I was "good," God should be good to me. I held on to my religion because times were tough for me in the Marines and I thought I could use God to get me through it. Then, after things were better, I could just go back to my old way of life. That is, of course, exactly what I did.

My time in the Marines was a rough period at best. I entered Boot Camp at the age of seventeen. I was not yet ready mentally for the rigors of military life. I was very immature and basically felt like life "owed me" something.

This was clearly the wrong attitude to have and it didn't serve me well. As time went on, I fell into a deep depression. I finally reached the point that I was so confused that I had no idea who I was anymore. I wasn't able to keep up the appearance of being "religious" any longer, nor could I pretend to be a good Marine.

I didn't even want to be a Marine anymore. I didn't want to be anything. I wasn't even sure that I wanted to live. I began to question my reasons for everything and shortly thereafter, the drinking started again—and this time it *really* started.

It was perfectly normal for me and some of the guys in my platoon to each drink about a case of beer *before* leaving to go hit the bars. We would be dismissed at about 5:00 PM and by 7:30PM; I had usually downed more than a half case of beer.

Later we would go to town and start bar hopping. I will not even try to go into the kind of things that happened during those nights. To say that we were completely out of control is putting it mildly. We fought; we undressed in public; we stole; we destroyed property. You name it, and it happened.

My depression got worse and I eventually ended up in the naval hospital. They diagnosed with a "personality disorder" and I was discharged from the military. I was awarded an honorable discharge, but with no possibility of ever reenlisting.

After only nineteen months of service, I was out of the military and on my way home. I felt like a failure and, in many ways, I was. It was not because the military didn't work out, but because I was a phony and I knew it. I had gone through with my decision to enter the military, despite the fact that many well-respected people had advised me against it.

I enlisted because I felt I owed it to Angus (my friend from Chapter VI) and because I thought it would "fix" me.

I thought it would get rid of some of the things about me that I didn't like. But I learned that there is nothing that can fix you or make you happy if you aren't happy with yourself.

You can't be happy with yourself if you are looking for happiness in external things such as alcohol, money, power, etc. I will discuss this in more depth later in the chapter.

Prior to my discharge from the military, many of the marines in my platoon were confused by my behavior. Now, don't get me wrong, they were not all that concerned about the things that I did while I was drunk. To them, that was normal because most of them acted the same way.

What confused them was that they couldn't figure out why I was drinking in the first place since I had seemed "so religious" before. They saw me drinking like a madman and said, "Hey, Nick...What's the deal? I thought you were religious."

Looking back, I should have replied, "I *am* religious, but I'm not spiritual." If you remember anything from this chapter, I want you to remember that religion without spirituality is dead.

The Bible says, "Faith without works is dead" (James 2:20). In recovery, you can't have one without the other. You can go to all the AA meetings you want, but if you don't have a spiritual connection with a Higher Power, the meetings won't help. ***Knowledge can't save you from Alcoholism!***

Furthermore, you can have a spiritual connection with God, but if you don't put it into practice through service to others, you will lose your connection as soon as the tough times come since you have not made spirituality your way of life. Just remember that you need both spirituality and selfless works to recover.

If I had only realized the magnitude of this profound truth at that point in my life, I might have found the path to recovery and God much sooner. However, like so many alcoholics before me, I still had a lot to learn before I was ready to be truly free.

The second time that I quit drinking was during my first marriage. About five months after I was discharged from the Marines, I got married. My wife was very religious and, once again, I put away the bottle and picked up religion as a substitute. However, just like before, I didn't practice a spiritual life. Instead, I was a religious phony. I did not practice what I preached.

Everything about me was a lie. All of the behavior patterns that I had manifested while I was in the Marines came back. I was focused on myself rather than on others. I considered myself better than most because of my actions and, therefore, good enough in God's eyes. I was judgmental and I was a hypocrite.

I was a nightmare to live with. During my short marriage, I was completely unpredictable. My temper was out of control. I had virtually no patience with anyone, especially my wife. I was dishonest, hurtful, bitter and unforgiving.

It was only a matter of time before the practice of religion failed to adequately disguise my true self. I began drinking after about eight months of marriage. With the drinking, the intensity of my eating disorder increased. I practiced bulimia as a way of trying to maintain my weight when I was in the Marines and it became much worse when I drank.

Both my drinking and my bulimia became more severe as the days went by. After about thirteen months of marriage, my wife and I separated and, a short time later, we were divorced. I take all of the responsibility for this. I did nothing to stop it and virtually everything to cause it. My ex-wife deserved nothing that I put her through.

I was uncaring, unloving and unforgiving and I still didn't believe that alcohol had anything to do with it. I blamed everybody but me. I spread vicious rumors about my ex-wife, her family and her friends. I believed that I was normal and everybody else was screwed up. Looking back, I can see that I had a lot of learning and a great deal of growing up to do.

I hope you now understand that alcoholism exists, even when you aren't drinking. Just because you put the bottle away doesn't mean that you have recovered. You must get rid of your character flaws to achieve full recovery. Some of the meanest and most hurtful people I have ever met don't drink alcohol. Some of them never have. But that doesn't mean that they are good, healthy people.

If you are an alcoholic that has quit drinking but isn't working the steps, I can almost guarantee that you will go back to your old master, alcohol. It is only a matter of time before life becomes too much for you. That is why you need a new master, a Higher Power. Belief in a Higher Power is crucial to the success of your recovery and your completion of the steps.

Your Higher Power will remove your defects of character, but *you* have to work the steps. This doesn't mean that the Twelve Steps are worthless or unnecessary. Every component of recovery is important, but you can't neglect your Higher Power for the sake of the steps, nor can you neglect the steps to lay everything on your Higher Power. You must rely on your Higher Power *as* you work the steps. There is an old saying that goes something like this:

> "Pray as if it all depends on God, and act as if it all depends on you."

This is a good attitude to have in recovery in order to find the balance between working the steps and relying on God.

Unfortunately, there are many people in today's society that make serious mistakes in their understanding of what it takes to recover from alcoholism. In one camp you will find people who believe that if one would just "get right with God," then everything would automatically be okay.

They stereotype most alcoholics as "un-churched" and "faithless" people. They refuse to acknowledge that alcoholism is a disease. Instead, they call it a "symptom" or "consequence" of one's behavior. By that rationale, one could reason that adult diabetes that comes about from poor eating habits isn't a disease either. The same could be applied to the cancer that results from smoking.

Granted, these diseases do result to some degree from one's behavior, but that does not mean that they are not diseases. I suppose these people must also believe that someone with cancer or diabetes should simply "get right with God," and that that would take care of their condition. How ridiculous!

The belief that "getting right with God" automatically fixes everything is laughable. My Higher Power did not drive me to my Twelve-Step meetings. My Higher Power did not make my list of character flaws for me.

My Higher Power did not make me call my sponsor when I was in danger of drinking again. My Higher Power did *help* me to do these things by giving me strength and courage, but He did not *do* them for me. I had to work my steps. I had to pray daily for strength. I had to deal with problems without the aid of alcohol.

I had to learn to celebrate without alcohol. I had to learn to grieve without alcohol. I had to learn to LIVE without alcohol! Welcome to recovery! Without my Higher Power, I never could have done it, but my Higher Power didn't do it for me.

Along the same lines, you will find people who believe that once God is in your life, everything instantly becomes perfect. I am totally amazed that this belief so often comes from people who call themselves Christians and read the Bible, because this idea is completely unbiblical.

You can search the Bible from front to back, and you will not find anyone who didn't suffer after choosing to follow God. Noah endured the flood and became a drunk. Moses wandered in a desert for forty years before dying, having never entered the Promised Land.

David committed adultery and murder and lost his son. Job, the most righteous man on earth during his time, lost everything for a while. Ten of the eleven faithful disciples of Jesus were martyred and John was exiled. Paul, the author of most of the New Testament, was martyred.

The list goes on and on. Let it suffice to say that choosing God does not always equal a simple and carefree life. Such is also the case with recovery. Letting God, or whomever you choose to call your Higher Power, come into your life and help you recover is not always going to be comfortable, fun or convenient, but it will be worth it. You can choose to be a slave to your Higher Power or a slave to alcohol. Life is better with a Higher Power, but it isn't always easier.

Finally, there are those who want to take the spiritual element out of recovery. They try to view alcohol as simply a scientific or medical problem. They try to use science, logic, or medicine alone to figure out the reasons behind the disease and then come up with a logical way of 'curing' it.

Their motives are rooted in secular and humanistic beliefs that put the created above the creator. Ultimately, these people fail time and time again. I have seen some of their programs firsthand; they generally don't work. It amazes me that people with a lot of letters behind their names can't figure out why. I don't have a lot of letters behind my name but I am smart enough to know why these programs often fail.

These programs are designed based on the principle that truth is relative and subjective. Often times they are set up in ways that say what is good for one person is not necessarily good for another. Whether or not you agree, the reality is that this approach allows room for the alcoholic to make their own decisions about what they think is best for them instead of being accountable to a Higher Power.

I'm sure you see where this is going but in case you don't, here it comes. The reason these programs rarely work is because ALCOHOLICS ARE SELFISH!!!! If you allow us to we will ALWAYS put ourselves and our addiction first!!!

Programs that don't include belief in a power greater than ourselves allow us to set ourselves up as our own god. If we don't believe in a Higher Power that loves all of us (including those we have harmed) then we will put ourselves first and our selfishness will continue to grow unchecked.

We will do anything to get our drug. It is only by humbly allowing a Higher Power into our lives that we begin to understand that it is not "all about us." The world does not revolve around us and our addiction. We learn to acknowledge a power greater than ourselves and, more importantly, greater than our addiction. This teaches us humility. Once we have humility in our lives, compassion isn't too far behind.

The big blue AA book states that no human power could restore us to sanity. Believing this is absolutely essential to recovery and is, in my opinion, the most profound statement of AA. It *IS* the whole premise for the program. If no human power can restore us, then where is our hope? It *must* be in a Higher Power.

Millions of alcoholics through the years have been smart enough to figure out the simple fact that alcoholism is baffling. Yet countless doctors, scientists, social workers, corrections staff, hospital interns, treatment specialists and state officials that I have met over the years can't seem to grasp this simple truth (although there are many that can). It seems to me that man will go to any length imaginable to ignore or deny the existence of a Higher Power and his dependence on that power. I am reminded of a quote by St. Augustine written in 396 A.D.;

"We have been shown to what fragility man has been reduced by his own fault, and from what fragility he is delivered by divine assistance."

What is the point of all of this? It is simple. You can't pick and choose what parts of recovery you will and will not do if you truly want to recover. You cannot take the spiritual component out of the program and you can't take the program out of the Higher Power. You must work the steps with your Higher Power at your side to make sure that you are doing each step to the best of your ability and for the right reasons.

When it was finally time for me to complete Step Seven, I spent a lot of time thinking about whether or not I was being totally honest in my recovery. In Chapter Six, I talked a lot about the importance of being clean of heart and how important it is to have the right reasons behind the things we do. I knew I had to be clean of heart in order to come up with an honest list of character flaws. If my heart wasn't pure as I made my list of character flaws, then I would not be able to trust the accuracy of the list.

By looking back at the times in my life that I was a "dry drunk" and then comparing them to the times I was drinking, I was able to come up with a list of character flaws that were present with or without the influence of alcohol. Furthermore, in making sure that I was "pure of heart" by being honest with myself, I knew I could trust my list. When I was finally finished with my list, here is what I came up with:

My Character defects:
Selfishness
Greed
Lust
Jealousy
Hate
Anger
Bitterness
Insecurity
Unforgiving
Critical of others
Lack of Compassion
Pride

All of these character defects were causing conflict and contention in my life. The more I studied this list, the more I began to realize that something was missing in my life, something that all recovering alcoholics strive for and the one thing that only a Higher Power can give.

The thing I am speaking of cannot be purchased by money and it cannot come from material wealth. You cannot touch it; you cannot borrow it; you cannot obtain it through a faithless adherence to religious practices (although sincere religious practices can enhance it). It cannot come from a bottle; it cannot come from sex. It can only come from God.

The thing that I was missing was serenity, also often referred to as "inner peace." My life was utterly devoid of inner peace because I lived in a constant state of contention. When I completed Step Seven, I finally found that peace. As I continue in my recovery, I am becoming a peacemaker.

The seventh Beatitude from the Sermon on the Mount states,

"Blessed are the peacemakers, for they will be called children of God."

You cannot become a peacemaker if you are full of character flaws that stand in complete opposition to peace. By completing Step Seven, I not only discovered a rich and fulfilling inner peace, but I am now able carry it to others. My life reflects it, because my heart and mind are now filled with it! You can experience this for yourself when you complete Step Seven.

Once I realized this, I could not believe how perfectly placed this Beatitude was within the Sermon on the Mount. It couldn't have come any earlier in the sequence, because we wouldn't have been ready for it yet. If *any* of the previous six Beatitudes were not in place, then we would come across a roadblock to prevent God's peace from being able to flow through us.

Likewise, if we allow any character defects to remain a part of us, we will encounter a stumbling block on the path to serenity. Think of yourself as a bucket full of God's peace: If you lack or ignore *any* of the previous Beatitudes or recovery steps, then you will put a hole in your bucket that will drain unused serenity and peace away from you.

Today, I consider myself a "peacemaker in training." I do my best, with God's help, to practice my new way of living. I fail often, but I never turn back to alcohol. I have spent many years practicing life the wrong way and I know that it will take me a few years to get this new way of living down.

If I am ever unsatisfied with the new me, I can always go back to the old. I'm sure that alcohol would be more than happy to have me back. But today, I choose to live for God. Today, I choose to have peace, because I know from experience that God's way is better than mine, even though it is sometimes harder. I don't know what will happen tomorrow, but I do know that today I don't have to drink.

That is because the power of God's peace is more intoxicating than anything that comes in a bottle. If you are ready for this, take your list, drop to your knees and ask your Higher Power to remove your character defects. Your Higher Power *will* remove them and *will* help you to practice living without them until your *new* way of life becomes *your* way of life. Do it today. You are worth it!

Recovery is all about living your life without having to hide behind alcohol.

Chapter VIII

Step Eight: [We] made a list of all persons we had harmed and became willing to make amends to them all.

One of the most common phrases that you will hear repeated in AA meetings is "one day at a time." There are a lot of catch phrases that alcoholics in recovery use and sometimes we use them so much that we forget to stop and think about what they really mean. It is important to remember that these phrases all have meaning and are important. It is especially important to remember this particular phrase, "one day at a time," when you begin Step Eight.

I can't speak for all alcoholics, but for me, it was very important to know the reasons behind the steps. After reading each step, my first question was always "why?" *Why* do I have to do it? *Why* is this going to help? *Why* do I have to do it this way?

My sponsor would shake his head and reply, "Why don't you just shut up and do it?" In this book, I have tried to explain what I understand to be the reasons behind the steps, and one of the worst mistakes you can make when you begin Step Eight is to start jumping to Step Nine too soon.

I understand that it is human nature to ask, "Why do I have to make a list?," but Step Nine gives you the answer: Because you are going to make amends and that can be terrifying. However, you can worry about Step Nine on another day. Do not let your fear and dread of Step Nine prevent you from thoroughly completing Step Eight.

I know from personal experience that this is easier said than done, but try to focus on what you need to do today. You will have plenty of time to worry about tomorrow when it comes.

When I began Step Eight, I actually broke it down into two different steps. First, I focused on making a list. Then I worked on becoming willing to make amends. It was important for me to take this step and break it into smaller steps, or I would never have gotten through the first half.

Every time I started working on my list, I would think of someone that I had harmed. Then I would think ahead to the "making amends" part. Instantly, I would start coming up with reasons why I could never approach this person or that person again, let alone make amends to them.

In some cases, I would even convince myself that I *shouldn't* apologize to the one I had hurt. I would tell myself that I hadn't really done anything wrong. I would instantly become the nine-year-old who says to the playground teacher, "Well, he started it!"

As alcoholics, we are great at shifting the blame, and I was an expert in the field of dodging responsibility. I would remember someone that I had harmed and write their name down in my notebook. Then I would start getting nervous at the thought of apologizing to them.

Immediately, I would begin coming up with reasons why everything that happened with that person was actually their fault. "They had asked for it. They were mean to me first. They shouldn't take things so personally. I was drunk and didn't mean it," would go through my head over and over.

The list of excuses would go on and on in my mind and I spent weeks struggling against this roadblock while trying to complete Step Eight. To get through this step, I had to break it down into smaller steps in order to prevent myself from continuing down this path in my head.

A good example of my ability to shift blame onto others can be found in the way I treated my wife. All the years I was drinking, whenever my wife or someone close to me would confront me about my alcoholism, I would effortlessly begin to shift the focus of the argument onto them and their weaknesses or problems.

After a few moments of talking, my drinking was no longer even a part of the discussion. Eventually, the focus was all on them. I did this constantly with my wife as well as with other family members. At the end of many of these arguments, particularly those with my wife, I would walk away feeling fine, while she would walk away angry and feeling horrible about herself.

You may be reading this, thinking, "Wow, you were really an *a**hole*." All I have to say is that you are absolutely right!

Unfortunately, it wasn't just my wife that I did this to during my drinking days. Believe it or not, there were actually times in high school that some of my "drinking buddies" approached me about my drinking. How crazy is that!

My friends that I partied with actually came to me because they were concerned about my drinking! However, I never listened. I just turned it all around and back onto them and their own drinking. Many of these conversations with friends actually took place at parties!

There we were, a bunch of teenagers all standing around a keg, beers in hand, and my friends were telling me, with all the love and compassion that only a drunk can muster, that they were worried about how much I drank. They told me that my behavior while drinking was getting out of control.

This led to many very interesting arguments at parties, which then led to more drinking, until we had all drunk so much that we forgot what we were arguing about. At that point, we would just start professing our love for each other and go out to find more beer.

Many similar conversations even took place with drinking buddies as I got older. I can't tell you how many times I had friends who took me out for a beer to talk to me about my drinking. Oddly enough, I did the same thing with other friends on different occasions. What a bizarre disease!

My tendency to shift blame about my drinking did not go away just because I was in recovery and working the steps. I still had to be aware of it. Step Eight was a great exercise in taking responsibility for my words and actions and the effect they had on others. It was also a great step to practice taking things one day, or even one step, at a time.

In order for me to be completely honest with myself and truthfully complete Step Eight, I had to take it slow. When I was ready to begin this step, I went down to the drugstore and bought a new notebook and pen and began compiling a list.

At the direction of my sponsor, I began my list as far back as I could remember. I didn't simply limit my list to people I had harmed during the years I drank. I went back as far as kindergarten and began making a list of every person I had ever harmed, hated or held a grudge against.

I strongly encourage you to do the same and to use the same guidelines. Your list should include everyone in your life that you have ever harmed, hated or held a grudge against. There is a good reason for this, as you will soon see. Just remember the three H's:

Harmed   **H**ated   **H**eld a grudge against

Needless to say, my list nearly filled up the entire notebook.

I know that many of you reading this may wonder why I went back so far in my life to do this step. I asked my sponsor the same question when he told me to do it this way and he told me that, if you are trying to root out a disease, you must remove it all or it will come back.

Think of your alcoholism like a cancerous tumor. In order to be sure you are safe, the doctor has to make sure he removes it **ALL**! This doesn't mean that you are necessarily going to go make amends with every single person on the list as far back as your days in preschool.

However, it is important to be thorough in the list, because it will bring to light patterns of thought and behavior in your life that you may not have realized you possessed. Also, you don't want any unresolved baggage floating around in your head or in your past. It is best to deal with it all now so that you don't have to confront it again later!

As I began making my list, I started by focusing on people I had harmed. For me, I had harmed most people verbally. Some of you may have people on your list that you have harmed in a physical way. For me, the people I had hurt the most were the people that I had said hurtful things to or that I had said hurtful things about (gossip).

When I think back to the times in my life that I have been hurt, physical harm rarely comes to mind. I have been hurt the most by things that were said to me or about me. Those are the times that I remember most vividly. Physical bruises heal quickly, but emotional harm leaves scars that rarely fade. I know that I hurt a lot of people with my words and I cannot stress enough how much power our words have over other people and their feelings.

There were many times that I began to cry while I was making my list, not because of my own pain, but because I was beginning to realize how much harm I had caused certain people by what I said to them or about them.

While making my list, I began to see a pattern in my life; it was a cycle of hurting. People said things to me that hurt, and instead of responding with forgiveness, compassion and love, I responded with hate. In responding this way, I taught myself to be a bitter and vengeful person.

Had I responded differently (with forgiveness and love), I would have taught myself charity.

As I thought and prayed about this while making my list, I began to realize for the first time that I was no better than the people I had hated the most, those who had hurt me. I don't know why I couldn't see this at the time!

I knew how bad it felt to be hurt, and the last thing I wanted was to make someone else feel as bad as I did; but there I was, doing the same thing to others and it all started with words. WORDS! People said things to hurt me, so I responded by saying things to hurt them. I got so good at it that it became a way of life. Before too long, I wouldn't even think twice about saying something that would hurt someone's feelings.

From there, it was easy to begin gossiping. I no longer needed to be face-to-face with someone to hurt them with my words, I could do it anywhere with anyone! All I needed was my words. If I ever felt bad about hurting someone's feelings, all I had to do was drink and my conscience would numb up quickly.

While drinking, it was even easier to hurt people with my words because I didn't care! The alcohol not only numbed my conscience but often removed it completely. This is no way to live, but it is without a doubt an easy way to die. It really is a way of living that leads to death: the death of relationships, the death of happiness, even the death of your soul. The good news is that you don't have to live this way. You can recover. You can learn a new way of living. Welcome to recovery!

All of these feelings came to the surface while I was making a list of people I had harmed. By listing those people that I had harmed with my words and actions, I was able to begin to recognize the people who had harmed me.

Many times, these people ended up being placed on my second list: people whom I have hated. I hated them because they had harmed me. They had said or done things to me that hurt so badly that I simply hated them. They had done things that I believed that I could never forgive.

However, I quickly realized that I would soon be asking forgiveness from people that I had hurt just as deeply. I only hoped that the people on my list would forgive me. This led me to realize that I needed to be willing to forgive the people who had hurt me, if I expected others to forgive me.

This was not an easy thing for me to do. I spent many hours looking over my list and thinking about the people on it. I prayed about my list and, eventually, I was even able to pray for the people on it. I especially prayed for those people whom *I had hated or held grudges against.*

Over time, those people began to receive more of my prayers than the ones I had harmed directly. I became less and less nervous about making amends with those I had harmed and more nervous about making amends with those whom I had hated or held grudges against.

I realized, with much prayer, that the toughest part of this step is found between the lines. Making a list is fairly easy and becoming ready to make amends isn't too tough after you realize that the people you hurt felt the same way that you did when others hurt you.

The toughest element of this step, however, is learning to forgive the people that you hated or held grudges against. It is in doing this that I found real spiritual growth. When I was able to forgive the people I had hated or held grudges against, my whole life changed. Just when I thought I couldn't get any "higher" spiritually, my Higher Power blew the roof off my recovery when I was able to forgive those who had harmed me. I was taken to a whole new spiritual peak that was one hundred times higher than the one on which I previously stood.

I find it fascinating how recovery is so much "about me" and not others. I have stressed that in several parts of this book, but it is important to never forget it. Recovery starts and ends with you looking at yourself. You have to take responsibility for your own garbage. Blaming others, holding grudges, hating and dodging responsibility have no place in true recovery. Once I was ready to forgive others, I was also ready to ask for forgiveness from those I had treated badly.

I believe that there are some basic truths that are universal. They can be found in many places and in different belief systems and religions around the world. The idea that you must be forgiving in order to be forgiven is one such truth. The fifth Beatitude from the Sermon on the Mount reads:

> "Blessed are the merciful, for they will be shown mercy."

Throughout this book, I have been including some discussion on the Beatitudes and how they relate to the Twelve Steps. I believe that the truths found in the Beatitudes are universal as well. Whether or not Jesus is your "Higher Power" doesn't matter. For the sake of this book, what matters for recovery is that you recognize the truths found in the Twelve Steps and that these truths are also found in other places such as the Sermon on the Mount.

I have already discussed several of the Beatitudes (including the fifth Beatitude) in previous chapters but the fifth Beatitude (first mentioned in Chapter V) comes back into play again in Step Eight. No matter what you call your Higher Power, one quality that your Higher Power must possess is mercy.

God is merciful to us; our job is to forgive others as our Higher Power forgives us. Remember, we do not judge. Judgment is for God alone. As we forgive others, God's mercy is able to flow through us into other people. We learn to forgive, love, and show compassion. Hatred and bitterness become words of the past.

We are no longer people who add to the pool of vengeance and anger in the world that is already overflowing. We are now instruments of God's mercy. We become people that lift others up instead of tearing them down. We spread peace instead of conflict. We hold each other up instead of holding grudges. However, if the first seven steps or the first Beatitudes aren't in place, we will not be effective at accomplishing this.

We must work through the first steps in the order they are given by cooperating with God and letting Him work *through* us. This allows us to be truly ready to do what must be done when we arrive at Step Eight.

Remember that forgiveness is real. It is powerful and it is life-changing. When you are able to confess all your wrongs to another person (Step Five) and have that person tell you that you are okay and not judge you, it is an amazing feeling.

Why wouldn't you want to share that with others? Our first real taste of mercy comes at Step Five, but in Step Eight we are setting ourselves up to experience mercy in two ways when we get to Step Nine.

Make the decision now to forgive those that you hate or are holding grudges against, so that you will be ready to receive forgiveness from those with whom you are going to make amends. In making amends with them, you will be asking for forgiveness from them. Many, if not most of them, will freely give you forgiveness. But in order to really receive it, you must be willing to give it. You can do it. You are worth it!

Step Eight was a great exercise in taking responsibility for my words and actions and the effect they had on others. It was also a great

step to practice taking things one day, or even one step, at a time.

Chapter IX

Step Nine: [We] made direct amends to such people wherever possible, except when to do so would injure them or others.

The Ninth Step is not the hardest step, although I will admit that the first time I read the steps, I thought that it would be the hardest. However, in the process of working through the steps of recovery, I realized over time that the Ninth Step was not going to be all that bad.

For me and many others, the First Step was pretty tough. Having to admit that you are powerless over something is not an easy thing to do for most alcoholics. The fearless moral inventory certainly wasn't a party, either. Nobody enjoys taking a good, hard look at their faults and problems. And finally, telling another human being everything you have ever done wrong is also not something that most people are lining up to do.

Nonetheless, I got through it, just as thousands of alcoholics had done before me. Because I did the first eight steps correctly, I was not intimidated too much when I reached number nine.

The Ninth Step is all about making amends with the people we have harmed. Making amends requires taking responsibility. There are several things involved in doing this. The first is generally an apology and the second involves repairing any damage that you may have done to each person, whether it be physical, verbal or financial.

Obviously, we can't go back and change what we did, but we can repair the damage that has been done to the best of our ability. This is part of taking responsibility for our actions and it is not optional. If we want to recover, we need to do some repair work. The third is making bold and positive changes in your life.

Some people that we approach in this step will not be convinced that our apology is sincere. Our hope should be that, in time, they will come to see that we really have changed. Our new way of living will not only be a beacon of light for other alcoholics, but also proof to others that we are a changed person and that we can again be trusted. Our new way of living is outward evidence of our internal conversion.

In order to successfully make amends with people, all three of these things must be in place. I have come to understand in all of this that there is an order of things—inside and outside the body, heart and mind—that must take place in order for one to successfully apologize to those we have hurt or offended and to regain their trust.

The Twelve Steps have been designed to encompass many of these things, both directly and indirectly. However, I think that there are still things I should write about, despite the fact that you are already doing some of them without realizing it.

The first thing that happens on the road to making amends and repairing relationships with others is that you realize that amends actually need to be made. You not only want to do this but you are willing to do it. This is a great example of the power of spiritual awakening.

As alcoholics, our first spiritual awakening comes with the first three steps. We recognize our powerlessness, we believe that a power greater than ourselves can restore us and we give ourselves over to that power. However, these are not our only spiritual awakenings on the journey of recovery; they are simply the first that we encounter.

They are what start us on the journey. It is a journey that will bring us both joy and pain; it is a journey that will teach us about love and suffering. It is also a journey that has both ups and downs, but what we discover over time is that the downs are never as deep as they once were.

As we continue on our journey through the steps, we discover our own individual faults, but at the same time we are learning about the love that God has for us. We become powerful because of our vulnerability! We are weak, but it doesn't matter anymore because we have accepted the fact that it is not us, but our Higher Power that is going to do the work through us.

When we are weak and want to drink, our Higher Power makes us strong. When we look at our list of character defects and think that we are worthless, our Higher Power says, "You are worth it!" When we want to quit, our Higher Power tells us, "Keep going." Eventually, this power working inside us awakens the need and desire to "make things right" in our lives and with those whom we have harmed.

As a result of this, we now not only recognize the need to make amends, but we become willing to do it and to do it right. After all, our Higher Power hasn't let us down yet, so why stop now? When we have reached this point in our recovery, naturally we find ourselves at Step Nine. Step Nine is where we put our desires into action.

The first action we take is actually making the list. When I was ready to do this, I took out the notebook that I had used when I made my list of all the people I had harmed and I took out the notebook that I had used to make my fearless moral inventory. I began going through both notebooks, ultimately making a new list of people in a new notebook, naming those with whom I was going to reconcile my past wrongs.

I also made a secondary list of people with whom I needed to set things right but felt that this may not be the right time because to do so might harm them or others close to them. One of these people was my ex-wife. I thought about her a lot when I made the list and, after much prayer and consideration, I decided that it wasn't a good idea to barge back into her life after she hadn't heard from me for so long.

The last time I had talked to her had been many years before and over the phone. The conversation had gone very well. She had told me about her life and her kids and we had a very positive conversation.

When I asked my counselor about whether or not I should contact her for the Ninth Step, he felt it was best to just leave things the way they had ended the last time we spoke, but if I ever were to run into her by chance that I should go ahead and make amends.

I thought about it and decided to take his advice. If you have anyone on your list that you are unsure about approaching, I strongly advise you to seek the guidance of your sponsor, counselor or spiritual advisor. As alcoholics in recovery, we recognize that everyone heals in their own time and sometimes we can do more harm than good if we approach someone who isn't ready to hear what we have to say, even if our intentions are good.

I also made a list of people to whom I wanted to apologize but did not know their names. For example, one year I went to watch my wife emcee a beauty pageant. She was a Beauty Queen in the Miss America organization in college (she still is in my eyes) and every couple of years she would be invited to emcee the pageant (that she had won in college) and also sing a few songs. I was drunk when I showed up, and I chose a seat next to a few friends toward the back of the nearly full thousand seat auditorium.

Throughout the pageant, I was making loud comments about the various girls participating such as, "Oh, this girl's a piece of work"; "That dress was a bad choice"; "Who told her she could dance?" etc.

When a contestant said something that I didn't agree with, I would boo her. I was constantly disruptive because I would use the quietest moments in the pageant as opportunities to explain to my friends in a drunken whisper (drunken whispers are never quiet) why this girl was going to place in the top four, or why that girl was an idiot, etc.

I considered myself an expert on pageants because I was drunk, and when I was drunk I was an expert on everything. Also, my wife had won the pageant in college and I was now married to her. Therefore, I was even more qualified to be an expert. I explained this to the strangers sitting behind me, as well; I'm sure they were thrilled.

The whole time this was going on, one of the ushers was trying to get me to shut up. Every time he would politely ask me to be quiet, I would respond by saying something like, "Go to Hell," or "Kiss my ass." I could tell that I intimidated him and I loved it. Since I began my recovery, I have constantly been on the lookout for that man. I don't know his name or anything about him, but I remember his face and I pray that someday I will run into him again. Until that day, he will remain on my list.

When I had finished my list, I went back through it and arranged the people in a specific order. I strongly recommend that you do this by putting the easier ones at the top of the list and the harder ones near the bottom. Doing this helped me gain confidence as I worked through the list. By the time I got to the hardest people, I felt unstoppable.

The second action we must take in this step is actually approaching the people on the list and making amends. Most of the time, this begins with an apology and, for most of the people on my list, an apology was all that was required.

To some, this might not seem like much, but a sincere apology goes a long way in restoring friendships and relationships. However, one of the things that I have come to understand in my own recovery is that an apology is not really an apology if you are going to do the same thing again. A sincere apology is more than words; the steps have taught me this reality. A sincere apology must be accompanied by the sincere intention of restructuring your life and correcting your unacceptable behavior.

That isn't to say that I wasn't, at least in some way, sorry for what I had done to different people during my drinking days; but how sorry could I really be if I fully intended to go on living the same way as I had before? An apology that is accompanied by an obvious change of lifestyle and attitude has real "weight" behind it. It is almost always appreciated, even if it isn't accepted at first by the person to whom you are apologizing.

Alcoholics are generally not very good at apologizing. This is crazy, because if you are anything like I was, you have done more than your share of what you thought was apologizing during your drinking days. I'm sure many alcoholics can relate with me on this when I say that I spent many mornings making phone calls to friends trying to apologize for my drunken behavior the night before, but without taking too much responsibility.

As an alcoholic, I had plenty of practice dishing out empty apologies to my friends, my wife, bar owners and others. Of course, that is all they were, empty words. My behavior never changed, and my apologies—even the ones I made as a very sincere drunk—were anything but sincere. They were totally devoid of sincerity because I fully intended to go on drinking. I had no plans to alter my lifestyle or to repair my bad behavior.

My apology was just a way of looking for a "ticket" to keep drinking. In other words, I wanted the person to say in response to my apology, "That's okay; don't worry about it." Every alcoholic loves those magic words, "Don't worry about it."

It is like giving us a license to go on drinking! I dished out hundreds of these types of apologies to people over the years because I knew that they would respond by telling me not to worry. I was especially good at offering these types of apologies to my drinking buddies, because the unwritten code among alcoholics is that you always had to accept your friend's apology.

Otherwise, someone might have to admit that they had a problem with alcohol and God forbid that we would ever do that! These hollow words could be offered to a fellow drunk for any indiscretion that occurred as a result of alcohol.

"Hey Bob, sorry about last night, I didn't mean to stick my head up your wife's skirt."

"Oh, that's okay Bill, don't worry about it."

I had uttered those magic words to my friends many times. I always forgave my drinking buddies, because I knew that next time it might be me saying, "Sorry about last night." And of course I would expect to hear the usual response, "Don't worry about it."

However, the people to whom I never apologized were the ones that I knew would never respond in a way that would give me license to go on drinking. Instead, I knew that they would hold me accountable for my actions and challenge me to do something about it.

They might lecture; they might ask me why I behaved that way; they might even make me think about my drinking. Of course, I didn't want that to happen. The last thing I wanted as an alcoholic was any kind of accountability.

But accountability is one of the key foundations of our recovery process. To begin with, we learn in recovery to be accountable to ourselves. One of the most repeated phrases in Twelve-Step meetings is, "To thine own self be true."

We must always be honest with ourselves if we hope to recover. Remember, recovery demands "rigorous honesty." If we can't be honest with ourselves, there is no hope that we will be truly honest with others. While in recovery we are also obligated to be honest with our Higher Power or God. We must be open with God about our powerlessness and be sincere in our belief that God can restore us to sanity.

Then we are called to be honest with ourselves again when we prepare our moral inventory. Next, we tell another person the nature of our wrongs. In this, we are again called to be honest. Throughout the Twelve Steps, honesty is required of us as the fundamental building block of accountability. Without accountability, there is no recovery. In Step Nine, for an apology to be honest, it must be sincere.

Despite the sincerity of my apologies, for some of the people on my list, an apology was not sufficient. In a few cases, I not only had to apologize, but I also needed to make further reparation in order to compensate for the damage I had done.

Making reparation is part of making amends, but it is not quite the same thing. For example, if I borrow a friend's car without permission and I damage it, there are several things I must do to make things right. The first is that I need to confess to my friend that I took his car without permission and apologize for doing so.

This is making amends, or "reconciling." However, our relationship is really not fully restored until I take care of the damage that has been done to the car. This is called making reparation. Once that is complete, then I can rest easy knowing I have done all that I could to make things right. All that is left to do beyond that is to not make the same mistake again, so that I can regain my friend's trust in me.

As I have already said, we cannot go back and change what happened, but we can do our best to restore our relationship with those we have harmed. In completing Step Nine, there were a few people that I not only had to apologize to, but I also had to pay back some money that I had taken from them.

In one case, I had to pay for some damage I had done to property. In both cases, I was overwhelmed at the compassion and understanding that these people showed to me when I confessed to them what I had done and offered to make it right. There was no judgment; there was no lecture. They just told me how proud they were of me.

One person even tried to keep me from paying them back, but I insisted. I told them that I needed to do this. If anyone is reading this who has stolen from friends, family or business, and you are nervous about approaching these people, all I can say is that it is worth it.

You may be very surprised by how well things go. Pray to your Higher Power before you approach them and trust that things will work out. As crazy as it seems, things really do seem to work out in recovery. Everything seems to happen at the right time. I don't believe that this is mere coincidence either. Instead, I believe that it is our Higher Power watching out for us. Even the steps themselves are in the perfect order and Step Nine is no exception.

The Ninth Step is perfectly placed within the Twelve Steps. If it had come any earlier, I wouldn't have been ready; if it had come later, it would have been too late. It is ideally placed in the sequence because, by the time we get to it, we are perfectly ready.

We are prepared to start apologizing and making amends with genuine sincerity. Now, unlike other times in the past, we are doing it for the right reasons. We want to make things right in every place that we can and we want to see broken relationships healed.

In my case, I actually wanted some people on my list to be able to get mad at me and to let me know, to my face, that what I had done had hurt them. I knew that they needed to do this so that they could let go of the past and begin to heal.

When I began approaching people to apologize, reconcile and repair our relationship with one another, I knew in my heart that it was the right thing to do. I also knew I was doing it for the right reasons. I had pure intentions behind what I was doing.

Basically, I was at peace with myself and my recovery and, as a result, I was clean of heart. I wrote about the sixth Beatitude in Chapter VI. It is strange that the sixth Beatitude readily applies to Step Nine as well. In fact, in Step Nine, we learn an even deeper spiritual truth about this Beatitude:

"Blessed are the clean of heart, for they will see God."

Being clean of heart means having the right motives and intentions in all of the things you do! Are you seeking God's glory through your actions, or are you seeking glory for yourself? Are your actions meant to lift someone up or help someone or are your actions meant to hurt or degrade somebody?

When I started making amends with people from my past, I knew I was not just doing it for my recovery. I was also doing it because I knew that other people had been hurt because of things that I had done or said. I wasn't just trying to make things right so that I would feel better and have a clear conscience, but I was actually considering the thoughts and feelings of those whom I had treated badly.

In many cases, I was putting their well-being above my own. I wanted to apologize so that they could move on. The very fact that I was thinking of them without regard for myself helped me to recognize that I was becoming clean of heart. I was actually doing good things for the right reasons!

As I discussed in Chapter VI, being clean of heart means having pure intentions behind the things that you do. When someone is clean of heart, they are not motivated by selfishness, jealousy, or anger. Instead, they are motivated by a desire to love, to have mercy and to reconcile. People who are clean of heart believe in true justice, not petty revenge. They put others first and they know what it means to love unconditionally.

The promise in this Beatitude is that we will see God. I firmly believe that this promise is fulfilled when we complete Step Nine. However, this time, seeing God means more than just seeing how He is working in your life (as in Chapter VI). When you complete Step Nine, you will actually see God face-to-face. You may be reading this and be thinking to yourself, "You are crazy! We can't see God!"

But if you have completed the Ninth Step with pure intentions, then I insist that you have seen God. You have seen Him because you cared enough about other people to seek them out and make amends. In order to really see God, you have to understand that "seeing God" has very little to do with a visit from some faceless celestial being. People who truly "see God" do so because they are able to see Him in others.

When we complete the Ninth Step, we are able to recognize that this "Higher Power" that created us and freed us from our prison of alcohol also created the people we harmed because of our drinking. We realize that by making amends and showing love to these people, we are also making amends with and showing love to God.

Do it today. You are worth it.

Throughout the Twelve Steps, honesty is required of us as the fundamental building block of accountability. Without accountability, there is no recovery.

*I have not talked much about my current wife in this book for a couple reasons. First, I don't wish to use my alcoholism as a tool to bring her into the "public eye." I don't know what it is, but every time a politician or public figure is caught with his proverbial pants down, it seems like the next day we always see him on TV standing next to his wife, the very person he victimized through his infidelity or misbehavior. I have a problem with this and I really don't want to do the same thing to my wife. I realize I am not a celebrity and that I am writing this book using only first names, but part of my responsibility as a husband is to protect my wife. This book is about my mistakes and my life, not hers. Second, this book is about my recovery, not my wife's ability to put up with an alcoholic. However, I will mention that my wife is an awesome woman who has put up with a lot. She has stood beside me despite my giving her many reasons not to. At the end of the book, you will hear more about her. Until then, she will remain an obscure character in the story.

Chapter X

Step Ten: [We] continued to take personal inventory and when we were wrong, promptly admitted it.

I have already written a lot about my inability to admit when I was wrong. I have written about how I believe that particular flaw found its way into my character and how it was often made worse by my drinking. I am not going to spend any more time writing about why this caused problems for me or how I overcame this particular fault.

What I would like to spend some time on, however, is how important it is to admit when you are wrong once you are in recovery and how being able to take responsibility for your mistakes will help you continue to stay sober.

By the time you reach Step Ten in recovery, you should be able to recognize that admitting you are wrong is something that is essential. It helps us to take responsibility for our mistakes and taking responsibility is always the first step toward making amends and restoring trust.

One of the most important character traits possessed by the people that I admire most is their ability to admit their mistakes and say, "I'm sorry, I was wrong." Because they possess this trait, they are also the people that I trust the most. If you are able to openly admit to others when you are wrong, you are actually making yourself easier to trust.

People suddenly begin to look at you as "the real article." You are no longer someone who makes excuses, blames others or dodges responsibility. Great leaders all share this trait. In some people I have met, it seems like this trait is so much a part of them that I sometimes wonder if they were actually born with it.

I trust these people in my life, because I know that, not only will they always be honest with me, but they will also never become too old or too proud to learn something new. These people make great bosses, spouses, friends and coworkers. They are always honest with themselves and with others and people naturally want to follow them, because they know that their pride or egos will never get in the way of their ability to make the right decision.

Consequently, on the other side of the coin, people who NEVER admit when they are wrong are usually not very much fun to be around. They are not easy to trust, because you never know when they may use you as a scapegoat for a mistake that they made. They make poor leaders, lousy bosses, irritating friends, obnoxious co-workers and contentious spouses.

They are often defensive and confrontational people; many times they are very self-absorbed and egotistical. They must be right at all costs. They are difficult to forgive and they seldom forgive others. They are uncomfortable to be around, because you are never sure if you are getting the truth from them on virtually any subject. I recognize that I was once one of these people.

It pains me when I think that many people used to view me in this way. Now, I am comforted by the fact that I have found a better path through the grace of my Higher Power. Of course, I didn't change overnight. I had to practice my new way of life in each step of my recovery.

I also had to practice the elements of this step for quite a while before they became something that I did naturally and without thinking. This included learning to take personal inventory of my actions. There are several ways that I found that are beneficial in helping me to do this and I would like to share a few of them with you.

One of the things that helped me the most in learning to admit that I was wrong was seeking the advice of people I trusted when I was faced with difficult decisions or situations. I cannot place enough stress on the importance of having mentors in your life. I don't care how old or experienced you are; you are never too old for a mentor. In

AA, the importance of a "sponsor" is often emphasized in meetings and literature.

There are good reasons for this. The first "good reason" that usually comes to mind for those of us with addictions is that we know how out of control we can become when nobody is aware of our sickness so having someone to "check in" with keeps us "in check."

However, once we are on the road to recovery, there is still much to learn. Just because we are sober does not mean we are safe. There is great wisdom to be had from people who have been down the same road before us. We should be humble enough to recognize that we don't know it all and be willing to take advice and guidance from those who have "been there and done that."

In my work with youth, I often find myself talking with parents and teens about their relationships. One of the most common phrases I use is this: *High School is the time that teenagers need their parents the most but talk to them the least.* Those of us in recovery can apply this statement to ourselves if we rephrase it to say, "Recovery is the time we need the wisdom and help of others most, but often fail to seek it because we are too proud or ashamed."

Ever since I entered recovery, I have had what I like to call a "spiritual advisor." During my first year in recovery, I had a sponsor, but I quickly moved on to a spiritual advisor. I wrote about Fr. Simon earlier. He was a grumpy Benedictine monk who had great love and compassion, despite his gruff persona, as well as an excellent ability to see through my BS.

The discussions that I had with him over the years were invaluable to my recovery and spiritual development. If you are a person of faith, I highly recommend finding a spiritual advisor from your own faith or denomination to guide you and keep you accountable as you continue to work on your recovery. If you are not a person of faith or have problems with organized religion, then simply finding a sponsor from your AA group to continue to meet with will certainly suffice.

There is also nothing wrong with having two or three people that you can call or meet with when things get rough or you need some special guidance. Also, don't hesitate to seek advice on things other than recovery. Remember that recovery is about living life, not just overcoming addiction.

If you are a teenager, I have some advice for you as well. One of the first things I suggest to teens who come and talk to me when they are having problems with ANYTHING (addiction included) is to make a list of five adults that they trust. They could be teachers, coaches, youth ministers, and friends of the family or whoever.

Then I tell them that I want them to contact these five people. I instruct the teen to tell these five people that they are going through some tough times right now and then ask them if it would be okay if they call them when they need someone to talk to when things get too hard to handle.

Once this has been done, the teen now has a list of, not one, but five people who can be lifelines of support when help is needed. For guys, I always suggest men, and for girls, women. I do this because of a saying I once heard. I don't know who said it, but I fully agree with it, "Boys become men in the company of men, and girls become women in the company of women." The premise is simple: Boys don't become men by hanging around other boys.

Unfortunately, there are a lot of adults out there from ages eighteen to ninety that are still stuck in their high school years. The best way to grow into a successful man or woman is to keep company with successful men and women. You will share the goals and beliefs of those with whom you surround yourself. Choose your friends wisely.

Another way to help stay on track with Step Ten is to make sure you pray or meditate every day. Do not ever lose contact with your Higher Power! Remember, God, or your "Higher Power" was the guiding force that restored your life to sanity. If God is powerful enough to restore sanity to an otherwise disheveled lifestyle, He is certainly strong enough to keep you sane and help you to continue growing.

Do not neglect your communication with, and prayer to, God. Maintaining contact with your Higher Power is part of taking personal inventory! Never forget that addictions are sneaky; they will find a way back into your life, just like a burglar will try to find a way past your home's security alarm system.

God is your personal alarm system and attack dog all rolled into one. Stay in contact with Him.

Many times, people have asked me, "What should I pray about?" Pray about anything! Pray about work, your problems, your hopes or your dreams. Take a daily inventory of your actions by discussing your day with God. Ask Him to help you see what mistakes you made that day and ask Him to help you to do better tomorrow.

This daily inventory is VERY important; it is part of being true to yourself and it will help you mend and rebuild your conscience, a conscience that has been damaged and clouded by years of drinking. In your prayers, you can also thank God for your successes that day, as well. Pray for your enemies. That sounds tough I know, but believe it or not, it actually works. Pray for other alcoholics. Pray for anything; just pray!

Pray for anything; just pray!

Prayer, in my opinion, is the pathway to peace. It can bring about an inner peace that helps us to know that things are going to be alright. It can have a calming effect on us and help us shut down our mind and fall asleep at night. For example, your evening prayer could be as simple as shutting off the light in your bedroom and, after taking an inventory of your actions that day, saying, "God, I've done my best today; things are now in your hands tonight. I'll see you in the morning."

This sounds funny, but for many people (myself included), it can be tough to fall asleep at night because you have so much on your mind. Try putting all this stuff into the hands of your Higher Power at night. You'll be amazed at how much easier it is to fall asleep.

Just as prayer is the pathway to inner peace, it is also the pathway to peace with others. As your inner peace increases through prayer and meditation, your attitude will continue to change. Soon, you will find yourself becoming a more content and peaceful person in your relationship with others.

Your inner peace will overflow into your actions and will affect others in a positive way. I think we could all agree that the one thing the world could certainly use is more peacemakers. However, everything needs to take place in order and it is all based on your continued contact with your Higher Power. When you pray, you demonstrate trust in your Higher Power.

With trust comes the willingness on your part to take personal inventory of your life each day so that you might mature in your recovery. Because you trust your Higher Power, you are willing to continue to make changes in your life. As you adjust your lifestyle patterns by admitting when you are wrong and seeking forgiveness from others, you in turn have a positive effect on those around you. Your inner peace becomes an outer peace that you are able to share. This process never ends, and it repeats itself every day of our lives.

The seventh Beatitude reads:

"Blessed are the peacemakers, for they will be called children of God."

Many faith traditions refer to God as a heavenly "Father," "Mother," or "Eternal Parent." If you do not view God this way, then that is fine. I myself do see God as a heavenly "Father." Regardless of what we call our Higher Power, I think that most of us in recovery would agree that our Higher Power is a completely loving power and is the source of our ultimate peace.

Therefore, when I read something like this Beatitude, I can't help but be reminded that children often turn out like their parents, because parents are usually their most influential role models. So it follows that if our Higher Power is an eternal parent full of love and peace, we should strive to follow that example so that we, too, may be full of peace and love.

By allowing our Higher Power or "God" into our lives, we are opening the door to a peace and serenity that is beyond anything we will find anywhere else. If we have worked the Twelve Steps correctly, we know that our lives are on the right track.

Therefore, we become constantly open to growing in peace and love. If we are open to this, our Higher Power will certainly use us to spread this peace to others. However, if we do not take daily inventory of our actions or we are still weighed down by our character flaws, then we are not open to continued personal growth and not able to effectively spread peace through our words and actions.

I can't speak for everyone, but I have found that being a peacemaker is one of the hardest things I've tried to do because, for so long, I had the wrong idea of what being a peacemaker means. I thought that it meant being an outspoken activist against the "evils" of society.

I thought that being loud and noticeable concerning pertinent issues in the public square was what a true peacemaker did. I have never been more wrong. Granted, there is a need, at times, to speak out against things when we are led to do so by our consciences. However, true peacemaking begins at home. It starts with your spouse, sibling or parent.

It moves from there to the person sitting next to you or the person living next to you. It branches out from there to your neighbors and co-workers. It grows in ever-widening circles into your community and state. From there, it gains momentum to cover your nation and the world. But it all starts at home.

You cannot bring peace to the world if you don't live in peace with those you are closest to. Also, you can't share peace with those you are closest to if you don't have a basic peace within yourself. The instant that "peace" or "serenity" leaves you; your recovery from alcohol is in jeopardy.

Step Ten is about maintenance and growth. Neither can come about without the peace and serenity that you receive from constant communication with your Higher Power. Remember to stay in contact with your Higher Power, take a daily inventory of your life and never be afraid to admit when you are wrong.

You are worth it.

Throughout the Twelve Steps, honesty is required of us as the fundamental building block of accountability. Without accountability, there is no recovery.

Chapter XI

Step Eleven: [We] sought through prayer and meditation to improve our conscious contact with God, as we understood Him, praying only for knowledge of His will for us and the power to carry that out.

It seems strange at this point in recovery to have to write about how important it is to stay in contact with God. However, it is important to maintain this regular contact with our lifeline and not let our guard down for a minute.

I remember a television special about stuntmen in Hollywood and the work they do. I was amazed at how much planning went into each stunt, no matter how small. Every detail was planned and taken into consideration. Every possible thing that could go wrong was discussed and contingency plans were made for each scenario.

The thing from that television special that surprised me the most was that they said that most accidents occur right after the stunt goes off successfully. In other words, people usually don't get hurt during the stunt when accidents seem most likely to occur.

It is usually immediately after a successful stunt instead. The reason for this, they said, is that people tend to let their guard down too quickly as soon as they see that the stuntman is okay. Then someone makes a mistake. When I started to work Step Eleven, I was reminded of how important it is to not let your guard down too quickly.

By the time you reach Step Eleven, you will have some sober time under your belt. It may be eleven weeks or eleven months; it really doesn't matter. The point is that you will have spent some time being sober and you will have developed some confidence in your recovery. This is good, but it can also be dangerous.

Do not let that confidence turn into pride or overconfidence. Those who allow their pride to take control are usually the ones who fall the hardest. I think that this is one of the reasons that Step Eleven is so important. Just as you start to get confident in your recovery, the steps direct you to improve your contact with God.

Constant contact with your Higher Power is the key to recovery. Every single step involves contact with your Higher Power. From the very beginning of the steps, when we admit we are powerless and need God, to Step Eleven where we are told to improve our contact with God, He is the source and the reason for our recovery.

For me in my recovery, what Step Eleven is saying between the lines is, "Increase your contact with God and do what you're told or else!" ("Or else," meaning you will return to alcohol.)

To be honest, by the time I was at Step Eleven I did need a bit of a kick in the pants to make me spend more time with God. I also needed new things to pray about. I had gotten into a routine in my recovery; every prayer I prayed seemed to focus on not drinking or having enough patience to not kill somebody.

I worked the steps, went to meetings and talked to my spiritual advisor who had introduced me to the Beatitudes. I was learning a lot through the steps about living without alcohol, but I still felt like the focus was on "not drinking," and I had begun to wonder, "What comes next?"

Step Eleven tells you how to find out what does come next. It pushes you to increase your contact with God and then tells you exactly how to find out what is next in your life by telling you to pray for God's will and the strength to carry it out.

When I sat down to pray about Step Eleven, I was under the impression that my recovery was almost over. I found that I was very wrong. My recovery and my life without alcohol were only just beginning. Now that I was sober and somewhat stable, it was time to find out how my Higher Power wanted to use me.

Being used by your Higher Power is the second part of Step Eleven. In Step Eleven, we are first told to increase our contact with God. But why? Shouldn't we already know that contact with God is important? There has to be more to this step than just spending more time with God!

The second part of the step reveals the reason that we need more contact. For the first time in our recovery, God is going to use us to directly help other alcoholics, but He can't do this unless we are open to being used by Him. Remember, recovery is not just about us.

Throughout the steps, other people have been involved directly or indirectly in our recovery, but when we complete Step Eleven, we are ready to actually bring new people into our lives. We are now ready to start helping other alcoholics.

However, before you can do this, you have to understand a few things. First of all, if you don't want to be used by God to accomplish great things, then don't ask for it. I promise you that by the time you get to Step Eleven, if you want God to use you to help other people and you ask for it, He will definitely grant your request.

Sometimes, this can be scary and it will often make you uncomfortable. But when I did it, I have to admit that it is the greatest high I have ever experienced! You may be thinking that you are not worthy to be used by God or that you couldn't possibly help anyone because you feel that your life is still a mess.

This is all a bunch of crap. Put those thoughts out of your head and look back for a moment at all the miracles that God has already accomplished in your recovery. You are sober. You have had your character defects removed. You have mended relationships. If God can do all that, then He can definitely use you to help others.

In fact, He is counting on you and so are the people that you are going to help. To put it another way, people that you have not even met yet are counting on you to help them! This is why your recovery is SO IMPORTANT! Other alcoholics are depending on you to recover and then come find them! To do this, you must let God direct your life.

You must let Him lead you to these people. It is not enough to just say you are willing to go. You must actually *"improve your conscious contact with God, as you understand Him, praying only for knowledge of His will for you and the power to carry that out."* Anyone can say that they believe in God or a Higher Power, but true believers *act*; they don't just *talk*.

If you are ready to be used by God, then you are ready for Step Eleven. When I was ready to do Step Eleven, I sat down in my living room and spent some time thinking about whether or not I was really ready to follow God's will for my life.

I eventually felt at peace with the decision to move forward, so I said a short prayer. I asked God to direct my actions each day and to help me see the direction in my life that He wanted me to take. Finally, I asked Him to help me to recognize His presence in my life so that I might better see which direction He was leading me.

When I finished my prayers, I felt as though something in my heart and mind had been finalized. Those feelings of selfishness that I had prior to recovery, and even during recovery, were finally gone. For the first time, I truly felt that it was not "all about me," but that I was genuinely open to sacrificing my comfort and convenience in order to help others. It felt GOOD. *I* felt good.

It is important to remember, also, that you don't need to ask God to reveal all of His plans for you. We don't need to know all that God has in store. What is important to us as alcoholics is that we are sufficiently aware of God's presence in our lives to recognize when He is telling us to do something.

For me, this is a daily thing. It can only happen if I pray every day. I look at God, not only as my Higher Power, but also as my friend. Just like we spend time talking to our other friends, we need to spend time talking to our best friend, God. If we don't, then we won't recognize His voice when He tells us to do something.

My constant contact with God involves a short prayer every morning, in which I dedicate my actions, thoughts and words to God and ask Him to direct and lead me throughout the day. I pray at lunch time (Catholic prayers at lunch time, usually a Rosary). In the evening I take inventory of my day and ask for forgiveness for my mistakes and strength to do better tomorrow.

I also thank God for the successes of the day. I have tried my best to maintain this daily routine ever since I did Step Eleven. I also spend a lot of time just talking to God when I'm driving somewhere or when I'm trying to make tough decisions. These are the things *I* do, but they don't need to be the things *you* do. What is important, as I have already said, is that you are in CONSTANT CONTACT!

About a week after I completed Step Eleven, when I told God I was ready to follow His will for my life, I had my first "answer" to this request. I wrote earlier in this book that I had competed in boxing and that I enjoyed martial arts.

One of the martial arts I participate in now is Brazilian Jiu Jitsu. It is a wrestling/ground-fighting art that I find enjoyable and challenging. As I was leaving the gym one Saturday after an especially grueling class, I realized I had not said my morning prayer that day. As I drove, I quickly said my new "Step Eleven prayer": "Lord, I dedicate this day to you. May my thoughts, words, and actions all glorify you. Please guide me today to do your will, and give me the strength to do what you ask. Amen."

As I finished the prayer, I was almost to the on-ramp for the freeway to head back home when I got this sudden feeling that I should go to confession because it had been a while since I had last gone. The problem I had with this feeling was that I usually went to confession at a different Catholic Church than the one where I worked. My priest was also my boss and, even though the seal of confession can never be broken, I was more comfortable confessing to a priest other than the one I worked for.

I quickly dismissed the thought of going to confession, because I didn't feel like driving another fifteen miles in the opposite direction from the way home. I resolved to go the following week after Jiu Jitsu class.

However, the feeling came back again that I should go to confession. This time, the feeling wasn't just that I should go, but also that I should go to a specific Catholic Church (there were five in the area). As hard as I tried, I could not shake the feeling that I should go, so I turned my car around and headed toward the city where this Church was located. The whole time I was laughing at myself for being so silly and thinking I should just turn and go home.

I arrived at the church about fifteen minutes before confession started, so I decided to walk down the hall to see if the youth minister was around. Being a Catholic youth minister myself, I knew all of the area youth ministers and the one at this church was a good friend of mine.

As I came around the corner, I saw that the door to Carrie's office was open and she was sitting at her desk. I said hello and she invited me to sit down. Before I could say another word, she asked a question that floored me. "Nick, what do you tell someone who is struggling with drugs and wants help?"

I just sat there and stared at her. She must have thought I didn't hear her, so she asked again. Finally, I found my voice and asked, "Why?"

"Well," she replied, "There is a young man here, about twenty-two years old, who has been talking to me for about thirty minutes. He is in the bathroom right now. He says he is addicted to meth and needs help. I have no idea what to say to him. Can you help?"

Suddenly it all became clear why God wanted me at that church that day. He had someone for me to help. I almost screwed it up by not going. I vowed to never again dismiss my strange inclinations as silly or unimportant, because chances are that it would be God talking.

The young man came back into the office and Carrie introduced us. I spent some time talking with him. As it turns out, God wanted him at that church that day, as well. He had been living at a crack house and wanted to get out of that lifestyle but didn't know how.

He asked his friend to take him for a ride somewhere and, as they drove past the church, he felt he should ask his friend to stop. He told his friend he needed to run into the church for something. His friend asked why and he just told him to wait. His friend said he wouldn't wait.

So in the end, the young man just told his friend to leave him at the church and he would take care of himself. He just felt that he needed to go into the church. Once inside, the only staff member there was Carrie. Carrie talked with him for a while, not knowing what to say or do. While all this was going on, I had been having my wrestling match with God about driving out to this church (thirty miles away from my house) and thinking that I was silly for doing it.

I ended up talking with this young man for about an hour; then I drove him to the crack house so he could get his belongings. He asked me to go in with him so that he wouldn't be tempted to stay and get high, so I did. After we got his things, I drove him to one of the local rescue missions that also provided drug treatment.

I stayed with him while he checked in. Amazingly, the man at the front desk was a recovering addict who had known this guy in jail. Coincidence or God? Believe whatever you want, but I know it was another fingerprint of God in this whole affair.

After he was checked in, I wished him luck and told him I would pray for him and then I left. I never made it to confession, but I'm pretty sure God forgives me for that.

This was my first post-recovery experience of being used by God. It was a little uncomfortable and inconvenient, but it was amazing. And it was amazingly simple! When God is in control, everything becomes clear. Things that you think are important cease to be important.

God helps you see what matters and what doesn't. I wish I could do stuff like this every single day. Maybe I can and I just haven't gotten there spiritually yet or maybe I do and I just don't realize it. Whatever the case may be, the fact remains that I WANT to be able to have encounters like this every day, but I can't unless I am in constant contact with God and am willing to allow Him to be in control. I have to remember that it is not all about ME.

If you are struggling with Step Eleven, I want you to remember one thing: You must do this step! People that you have not yet met are COUNTING on you to help them! The alcoholics/addicts who are still suffering are waiting for us to find them. Do this step today; you are worth it!

People that you have not even met yet are counting on you to help them!

Chapter XII

Step Twelve: Having had a spiritual awakening as the result of these steps, we tried to carry this message to alcoholics, and to practice these principles in all our affairs.

Step Twelve, like many of the other steps, has more than one part to it. When I was ready to begin this step, I was so excited that I had reached the last step that I didn't really pay a lot of attention to its details. As I read it, I completely ignored the first statement, "Having had a spiritual awakening as the result of these steps." I also managed to ignore the second statement, as well—"...we tried to carry this message to alcoholics..."—and instead focused initially on the idea of "...practicing these principles in all our affairs."

For a while I felt that, because I tried to practice AA principles in all my affairs, I had completed recovery. Then, from out of nowhere, I had a bad day—a *really* bad day. It was so bad that I had the strongest urge to drink that I had ever had since I had become sober. At first, the urge to drink really threw me off because even though I had only been sober for a few years, I really hadn't had any serious cravings for alcohol. This sudden urge really messed me up. It kind of reminded me of how I felt in my first boxing match.

I boxed for almost four years and during that time I competed in several Golden Gloves and USA amateur boxing tournaments. I remember training very hard for my first bout. When the night arrived, I felt ready. I was in shape, I had a game plan and I was mentally calm. I felt unstoppable.

My coach warned me several times that I needed to stay focused and I kept wondering what he was talking about. I felt great. I was never more ready. However, when the bell rang to start round one, I instantly forgot everything for about ten seconds. It was the strangest feeling in the world. I knew how to box, but for some reason, I forgot everything.

After taking a couple punches and throwing a couple of my own, I finally was able to hear my coach's voice shouting, "Settle down, Nick! Work the jab, circle to your right!" Suddenly, it all came back to me. The fundamentals I had drilled on for hours flooded into my brain and came to the surface. I quickly dispatched my opponent before the end of the first round. This strange paralyzing feeling never happened again in the ring, but I will never forget the fact that, for a few seconds in my first bout, I was completely mentally frozen.

This is exactly how I felt on that day when I had an almost overpowering urge to drink. For a few minutes, I forgot everything about recovery. A million thoughts ran through my head. "What do I do?" "I'm going to drink and ruin everything." "Help!"

And then, slowly, I regained control of myself and one thought came into my head: "Go to a meeting." It's amazing how important it is to remember the fundamentals of recovery. If all else fails, GO TO A MEETING!

Going to a meeting that night was the best thing that could have happened to me. I hadn't been going to many meetings and it was good to be back. It also reminded me that recovery is never finished. If you don't make recovery a part of your daily life, then the time will come when things get too tough for you to handle.

Your only hope when that time comes is that the foundation of your recovery is strong enough to see you through until you can get back on the right track. But why take the chance? It is better to keep recovery on the top of your list than to take the risk of having one "bad day" leading you back to drinking.

After the meeting that night, I went home and looked over the Twelve Steps. I felt that perhaps I had missed something. My "bad day" had scared me so badly that I honestly believed that I might have done something wrong in the Twelve Steps. I went home that night and began to go through them all, starting at number one.

As I read each step, I reflected on how I had completed each of them and whether or not I felt satisfied with the work I had done. I felt great until I got to Step Twelve. That was when I recognized that I had not really completed this step because I had been looking at it all wrong. I suddenly realized that this step is never really finished. I began to read it over and over and, as I read it, I began to meditate about each part of it.

The first thing I thought as I read it was, "Have I had a spiritual awakening?" Some days I felt like I was on a different spiritual plane, but other days I felt like the only difference between the person I am now and the person I was then is that I'm not drinking. But when I looked back at all that I had accomplished in my recovery and how much I had leaned on God for help, I realized that I had indeed "had a spiritual awakening."

In many ways, I was not the same person. I was sober, and I was happy. My life felt "cleaned up." My spirit felt stronger and my faith unshakeable. I treated others differently. I apologized more and overreacted less. In so many ways, I had found serenity.

Satisfied that I truly had experienced a "spiritual awakening," I continued reading the step over and over. The second question that came to mind was, "Had I really tried to carry this message to other alcoholics?" As I thought about this, I realized that carrying the AA message to other alcoholics had been a real challenge in my recovery.

I didn't want to come across as a religious zealot like those who show up at my door on a weekly basis with the message that only their church is the right one. The last thing I had wanted was to be "that guy" in my circle of friends. I was afraid that trying to tell them about AA would make it seem like I was judging them or condemning their lifestyle.

I have always felt that one's personal example is the best way to spread a message of hope. I felt that if I was seriously working my recovery, my actions would reflect it. I felt that others would notice something different about me and ask me about it.

I'm happy to write that this has in fact been the case. Though skeptical at first, many of my friends who drink have asked me how I quit and why I'm so happy now. When people ask me this, it gives me the perfect opportunity to tell them about AA.

I don't preach and I don't condemn their lifestyle. I simply tell them that AA saved me from alcoholism and that it can help them, too! Sadly, many of my friends have not explored this further and continue to drink heavily. That's okay. They are still my friends and I love them. Every night, I pray that some day they will have the desire to do whatever it takes to recover from alcoholism.

I also pray that when that time comes, if God wills it, I will be there to help them find their way to AA. But if they never quit drinking, they will still be my friends and they can still count on me to be theirs. I would never end a friendship with someone just because they drink and I don't. By not pushing AA down their throats, I have kept the door open with them so that, if and when the time comes, they will listen to what I have to say about AA and recovery.

If you are worried about how you are supposed to take the AA message to other alcoholics, I encourage you to do so first by example. If you are truly recovering from alcoholism, people will notice that there is something different about you and will ask.

Some of your friends may be very skeptical at first, but in time their curiosity will get the best of them and they will ask how you are able to stay sober. Once they ask, you will be able to tell them about AA. Just remember that when this time comes, you should not be pushy with them. You can encourage them and offer to take them to a meeting, but they have to make the decision for themselves.

If you "talk them into it," then chances are that they won't stay in recovery. The bottom line is that if someone is not ready to hear about AA, then there is nothing you can say to make them ready. Take care of yourself. Make sure you are working on your recovery and make sure you are staying in contact with your Higher Power so that, when the time comes to share the AA message, you will be ready.

As I continued to read Step Twelve, I moved on to the third part of the step which calls on us to "practice these principles in all our affairs." The more I thought about this, the more I realized that recovery is never over.

As this thought came to mind, I began to laugh. I found it rather humorous that Step Twelve is a step that never ends. How ironic! All through recovery I looked forward to "finishing" the Twelve Steps, only to realize that there is no end.

Step Twelve simply tells me that I must put all that I have learned from recovery into constant practice in every area of my life. Step Twelve says that no matter what I'm doing or where I am, I need to stay in contact with my Higher Power, make amends to others when necessary, admit when I'm wrong, weed out character flaws, be honest with myself and so on.

At first I thought to myself, "What a sneaky trick! How am I every going to feel like I'm 'finished' with recovery?" Then I realized that it actually made sense to embrace the outlook that recovery never ends. In fact, speaking for myself, if I ever felt that I was "finished," I probably wouldn't be too far from drinking again.

When this thought entered my mind, I got chills. I realized that this was exactly the situation I was in right then! I had been under the impression that I was finished with recovery and had cut back on meetings and such. Then one day, when alcohol was the furthest thing from my mind, I ended up having a really bad day.

Then it was followed by the worst craving to drink I had ever had and what happened? For a few minutes I forgot *everything* I had learned in recovery. Wow! This was God's way of showing me that I needed Him and I needed to stay active in working my recovery. It was God's way of reminding me that alcohol is always going to be around and the minute that I decide I'm finished and let my guard down is the very minute I will start drinking again.

Step Twelve reminds me that I will always be a recovering alcoholic and if I want to stay sober, I need to "practice these principles of recovery in all my affairs." I had been neglecting my recovery, as well as neglecting my fellow alcoholics in recovery, by not going to meetings. God had simply allowed me to experience a small taste of what could happen if I continued on this path.

Up until that day, God had been very faithful to me in keeping me from having severe cravings to drink. He had given me strength when I needed it because I had *asked* for it every day. I talked to God about my recovery and I allowed Him to be in control of my life. But slowly, over time, I began to believe that I had beaten the drink.

I prayed about it less and went to fewer and fewer meetings. I guess God finally decided that He needed to get my attention and so He did. I heard the message, loud and clear, and I am very thankful that He didn't get my attention the same way He did the first time, by coming Himself. I'm not sure I could have handled another visit like that one.

Anyway, the important thing is that I got the message. Once again I began every morning with my usual prayer of dedicating the day to God and thanking Him for my sobriety. I now make at least a meeting a week, sometimes more, and I am constantly asking God to show me how to help the alcoholic who still suffers.

I may make a lot of mistakes in my life, but never again will I make the mistake of believing that I am finished with recovery. In order to be honest with myself about my recovery, I have to recognize that it never ends. If I stop going to meetings or stop communicating with God, then I lose those things in my life that keep me honest, accountable and ultimately, sober.

As I close this chapter, I would like to write a little bit about the two fundamentals of recovery, honesty and accountability, and how they relate to this final step.

Step Twelve calls on us to "practice the AA principles in all our affairs." Honesty and accountability are two major principles of AA, but they are meaningless without action. The principles of recovery also call on us to do the right thing. Sometimes this means apologizing to others or admitting when we are wrong, but more often than not, it means being honest and/or holding ourselves or others accountable.

My observations since becoming sober have shown me that most people don't like being held accountable, and many people are uncomfortable with real honesty. I think the greatest compliment that anyone has paid me since I got sober is when a co-worker said, "Nick, I don't always agree with you, but at least I know where you stand, and I don't have to guess about what your real motives or intentions are. I appreciate that!" When I heard that, I was so happy. I was being honest with others and myself and people were noticing.

However, just because people were noticing that I was being more honest didn't mean that it made my life easier. Sometimes being honest is not only the *right* thing to do, but it is also the *hardest* thing to do. This is especially true if doing or saying the right thing is unpopular.

However, if we wish to stay sober, then we MUST be honest with ourselves and others. As soon as we start lying to others, it won't be long before we start lying to ourselves; and once we start lying to ourselves, then it won't be long before we are rationalizing our way back to alcohol. To make matters worse, if we go back to drinking, then who will carry the message of recovery to other alcoholics?! Honesty in all our affairs is foundational to our recovery and to spreading the AA message. Honesty in recovery is second only to a belief in a Higher Power.

I have to admit that, when I was drinking, I was a great liar. That particular character flaw didn't just go away overnight after I started recovery. I learned very quickly to be honest with myself in matters relating to alcohol and recovery, but the importance of "honesty in all my affairs" really didn't fully hit home until I had been sober a few years and had had the aforementioned "bad day."

Don't get me wrong; I didn't go around telling huge lies or defaming people's character or anything like that. But there were a lot of little lies about little things that I convinced myself really didn't matter. Looking back, I am amazed at how many "little" lies I could tell in a day without even trying.

Eventually, I learned that there are no little lies. They are all lies and the more you tell them, the more problems you create for yourself. I finally realized that if I was a liar about anything in my life, how could I possibly be sure that my recovery wasn't also a lie?

Eventually these little lies led me to tell myself that it was okay to miss meetings and ignore my recovery, until I eventually convinced myself that I was finished with recovery. We know what happened next. One very bad day almost got the better of me. So much for being finished with recovery!

After going through that bad day and recommitting myself to recovery, I decided that it was time to be honest about everything, even about the little stuff that I didn't think mattered. No more calling in sick if I wasn't sick. If I needed a day off, I just needed to say, "Hey, I need a day off. I'm tired." No more little white lies to my wife. If she asked me to do something, no more telling her I was busy at work if I wasn't.

I know that these sound trivial, but THEY ARE STILL LIES. More than anything else, when I die, I would like for people to remember me as someone who was honest "in all his affairs." I can't speak for all alcoholics in recovery, but for me, if I was going to believe my recovery was real, I needed to be honest everywhere and "in all my affairs."

I wish I could say that now, no matter what, I am always honest and always do the right thing, but that in itself would be a lie. However, I can say that I always TRY MY BEST to be honest and to do the right thing.

Sometimes I fail, and sometimes I succeed; but successes and failures have been a part of recovery since the very first step, so there is no reason for that to change now. I do my best to be honest regardless of the outcome and, as I already mentioned, sometimes this brings more heat down on me than if I had just lied or avoided the situation.

However, Step Twelve says to practice the principles of recovery in ALL our affairs, not just when it's easy.

This whole idea of doing the right thing even when others may get angry with you reminds me of the eighth and final Beatitude, which states:

"Blessed are they who are persecuted for the sake of righteousness, for theirs is the kingdom of Heaven."

To me in my recovery, this means, "Blessed are you when you are persecuted for doing the right thing." This

Beatitude, just like the twelfth step of AA, never ends. For your whole life, God is going to ask you to do things that you know are right, even though they are unpopular.

Your recovery demands honesty from you in a world that teaches you that it's okay to "lie to get ahead." Your recovery and your Higher Power demand personal accountability, and yet the world says, "Do whatever feels good, even if it hurts others." There is nothing easy about the demands of the Twelve Steps or the Beatitudes. They are counter-cultural; they are not the way of the world.

Given the opportunity, nine out of ten people will choose the *easier* way, but that is not *our* way. As alcoholics in recovery, we are *spiritual* people. We have had a "spiritual awakening." We live for personal accountability and honesty. We hold ourselves to a *higher* standard that comes to us from our *Higher Power*. Our sanity and our sobriety depend on it. It will not always be easy, but it will be worth it, because we are worth it. YOU are worth it!

Good luck in your new life!

It's amazing how important it is to remember the fundamentals of recovery. If all else fails, GO TO A MEETING!

Chapter XIII
From Nick's Wife

I love Nick with all of my heart and I feel so lucky and blessed that we made it through all of this. I thank God for coming in and rescuing Nick when He did. I am so proud of Nick for all he has been through and for the steps he has taken to live sober. I don't know if I could have done what he did. He is a strong person with a good heart and I am so glad he is using his experience to give others hope.

As much as I love Nick and am glad that things are working out for us, I did make some mistakes in how I dealt with his alcoholism. However, I learned a lot from my mistakes and my purpose in writing this last chapter is to tell you, the reader, some of the mistakes I made in dealing with Nick and his alcoholism and what I learned from them.

I hope that in writing what I have learned and the mistakes I made, that you won't make the same ones, or will at least recognize when you are making them and take appropriate action.

Before I share these things with you, I first want to tell you how I felt when Nick told me he was going to stop drinking. He had taken me over to his sponsor's house so that he could tell me along with his sponsor. We sat there at the table and I was in tears as he admitted that he was an alcoholic and was going to start recovery.

He went on to tell me how much he really drank which blew me away. I guess I didn't realize how bad it was, and to be honest, there was a lot of denial my part. You see, that was my way of coping. As Nick told me with sincere words that He was going to stop drinking, the first thought that came to my mind was, "I wonder how long it's going to last this time."

You see Nick had tried to stop drinking several times before. One time he made it 3 months without drinking, but just like the other times he went back to it. I went along with the meeting, but didn't get my hopes up. Don't get me wrong, I wanted to do everything I could to support him in this, but I just couldn't believe (because of past experience) that "This was it."

The reason I tell you this is because I know that a lot of you reading this have also gotten your hopes up only to be disappointed. Whether you are the alcoholic (not in recovery) or living with the alcoholic, it is important to not give up. There is hope.

Okay, now for the mistakes and lessons learned portion of the chapter. The first thing you need to know is that you should never go into a relationship thinking you can change the other person. As much as I wanted to be the hero and to fix Nick's problems, I couldn't.

I knew Nick drank when we were dating and he hadn't stopped drinking when we got married, so what made me think things were going to change 'after' we got married? Simply this; I thought I could *fix* him. I thought that if we just had more time together that it would work itself out. I mean, he couldn't do this forever...could he? I realized that nothing that I did or said could make Nick stop drinking. That was a decision he had to come to on his own.

The second lesson, and by far the worst in my opinion is that you shouldn't hold resentment towards anyone for any reason because it only hurts you. As I write this Nick and I have been married 11 years (4 of those years he has been sober) which means I spent the first 7 years of our marriage living with an alcoholic who was drinking (not in recovery).

It is important for me to emphasize that Nick wasn't a sloppy or angry drunk and he would never hurt me physically (although the people who cared about me weren't so sure) but right from the beginning of the marriage he pretty much checked out mentally, not doing what I thought a normal husband should do.

He wasn't around most of the time because of work, band practices and late night gigs with the band so I spent a lot of time alone. Although he had a job to help pay the bills and did his part around the house by doing his own laundry and, sometimes even the dishes, I handled paying the bills, taking care of household things and fixing things that needed fixed.

It wasn't my idea of fun, but it was all I knew so I did it. The sad part of all of this is that I began building up resentment towards Nick without even knowing it. This hurt our relationship because I started losing respect for him. I acted more like his mother than his wife. This was a mistake.

Since he has stopped drinking it is very hard to stop playing that role. In the last 4 years I have tried my best to learn how to be a wife instead of a mother. I am still trying heal myself and get rid of the resentment I have for Nick that has built up over the years.

I've had to learn how to let him take over and be in charge of things in the house and to look at him as an equal. However, the hardest thing I've had to work on is treating Nick with respect. I had lost respect for him a long time ago. It seemed like a daunting task to bring that respect level back up to where it should be, but if Nick went through all he did to get sober, and continues to work hard to remain sober, then I need to put that same effort into healing and learning to respect and love him. I'm lucky that he is now patient with me as I learn this new way of living just as I was patient with him when he was drinking.

The third lesson, which is not my favorite to tell but very important, is that there are support groups designed for family members of alcoholics and if you are living with an alcoholic you need to attend one of these groups.

Nick's sponsor told me that it was very important for me to do this and that it would help me as Nick went down this road. So I found a meeting in my area and I went. It wasn't a good experience so I never went back. Not returning was a very bad decision.

Although these meetings may not always be what one might consider "fun," they do help you to do some true soul searching, which I desperately needed, as well as help change things about your attitude which can be beneficial in helping the alcoholic in your life recover.

I guess I wasn't prepared for what happened at the meeting I attended. Not going back was a huge mistake and I still kick myself for it. Many things that I did made recovery more difficult for Nick because I hadn't learned the correct way to handle certain situations.

Meetings for me would have helped me not make these mistakes. I'm glad that Nick's recovery was in God's hands and not my own.

And lastly, talking and confiding in people who are very close to you can be a very big mistake. I learned my lesson the hard way. I caused a lot of division between Nick and my family with my talking.

This division has only recently started to heal. Your family and friends will almost always take your side because that's the side they are hearing. The person you are talking about instantly becomes the bad guy and then your family and friends go into "protect" mode. They want to save you from this evil person.

While they are good to be close to during this time and their intentions may be good, they are not the ones you should be spilling your guts to. They are also not the ones you should be going to for advice on what to do with the alcoholic in your life.

They may be more than willing to give you advice but the advice is not necessarily good. My advice would be to always seek help from a professional counselor, therapist, addictions specialist or from those in a support group who have "been there, done that" before ever going to a friend or family member. Friends and family are great to lean on for support but not good for giving professional help. I hope I drove that point home.

In conclusion I want to say that the last 4 years, although extremely tough, have been very rewarding because Nick and I are learning to be married all over again. We giggle about silly stuff, spend a lot of time together talking and we are learning things about each other that we never talked about before.

Always keep that hope in knowing that no matter where you are in this battle, it is YOU who can make a difference in the outcome by learning and living the steps set forth in this book.

Keep the Faith,
Beth